Running with Unicorns

What I learned from a lifetime of helping my sister with her mental illness

BY CHARLOTTE GIBSON

DORRANCE
PUBLISHING CO
EST. 1920
PITTSBURGH, PENNSYLVANIA 15238

Dorrance Publishing Co
585 Alpha Drive
Suite 103
Pittsburgh, PA 15238
Visit our website at *www.dorrancebookstore.com*

ISBN: 979-8-8881-2087-3
eISBN: 979-8-8881-2587-8

Running with Unicorns

What I learned from a lifetime of helping my sister with her mental illness

Dedicated to

My sister, Sandra Wengle for inspiring my search
and enriching my life

Table of Contents

Acknowledgements:

They say it takes a village to raise a child. It took many individuals to support both Sandra and the completion of this book.

I will always be eternally grateful to my sister, Christine Wengle and her daughter, Candice Salonia who were there both for Sandra and for our mom when I wasn't available.

Thank you, Rochelle Rabinowicz who typed Sandra's notes in 2006. We would discuss the content as we wondered how to present her challenges.

Rick and Dr. Ruth Gallop saw potential in my project and would refer, suggest and even revise wording. They were an inspiration throughout my writing.

Many thanks both for suggestions and criticism go to Carolyn Wilkers, M.A. Sillamaa, Isabel Hetherington and Lucia Saja who made me think, revise or come back stronger with alternate thoughts.

I appreciate Simon Townsend and Joe Dwyer for introducing me to the world of publishing.

Colleen Brotton, Shirley Gibson, Margaret Motz and Duncan Campbell had words of encouragement throughout the years that kept me returning to the manuscript.

Our children Lisa, Brett and family, Lori and family, Brent (B.J.) and family and Jason supported me through many years of investigation even though they had no idea what I was talking about. They kept me sane, smiling and strong.

Finally, my husband Barry supported me through both good and bad times as well as my many challenges. This book never would have been finished without his ongoing support, love and care.

Author's Note

I am rushing to get to Sandra's bedside. She is my youngest sister and has been living in a long-term care facility for eleven years. Sandra was diagnosed as having schizophrenic tendencies at age 22. That diagnosis flipped between schizophrenia and manic depression (now called bipolar disorder) over the years. In her early thirties, Sandra was savagely beaten by a group of boys who took her jacket and expensive running shoes. Her jaw was broken, and she was left for dead. At 54 years of age, the doctors who assessed her at the Clark Institute told me that she was suffering from dementia from the beating. At the time of admission, the "dementia" diagnosis was confirmed, and I was told that she would be with us for another three years. I have now been called because they feel that end of life is near.

I look around the room. At least four residents have come and gone in those eleven and a half years. The room is plain, sparse even, painted beige with two residents sharing each room. There is a beige curtain around each hospital-style bed to provide privacy. All rooms are furnished with a four-drawer dresser, a night table, and a locker for boots, shoes and clothes that need to hang. There are large windows facing south and one chair for guests.

As I rush in, Christine, our middle sister who is two years older than Sandra and five years younger than me, is sitting beside Sandra's bedside with her daughter Candy. Each of them is holding one of Sandra's hands.

I begin my routine chatter and say, "Sandra, it's Charlotte. You are so smart. You were right." I see her eyes widen ever so slightly and the left corner of her lip raises to form a grotesque smile. *And they say she doesn't understand anything.*

She has two brown teeth at most. Her body is wasted. She has not been able to walk or talk for more than seven years and has needed assistance with feeding for the last five of those years. She has been confined to her bed for over a month. I tell her that I brought the most recent draft of our book, and I am going to read to her.

Christine said, "I never talk to her. I just hold her hand."

I thought about how I made up songs that I sang to her. I talked about the past, her high school years, the fun we had together, her journaling and letters. She laughed at appropriate times and tried to sing along with me, making unintelligible sounds. Sometimes a tear fell down her cheek when I asked if she remembered friends and relatives who had passed. Sandra and I had a bond that crossed illness.

We had two older brothers who both died young from enlarged hearts. We never knew there was such severe heart disease in our family. Bob, the eldest, died at age 55, and Joe died at age 60. Our dad died from dementia in his 82nd year and our mom from colon cancer in her 71st year. I was an orphan at age 45, Christine was forty, and Sandra was thirty-eight. Christine and I promised our mom on her deathbed that we would take care of Sandra and each other. And so we did for the next 29 years.

Sandra died on July 23, 2019, with her sister Christine, her niece Candy, and me by her side. Sandra was in her 66th year.

I loved that brilliant, funny woman who helped mold the wonderful life that I continue to live. This book chronicles my struggles to cure her, to care for her, and, finally, to learn from her.

My journey led me into the world of long-term care where much change is needed both for the small population that I explored as well as for the countless individuals seeking admission in future years who do not currently fit into the mold of patients who our present-day caregivers have been trained to support.

I learned from supporting and advocating for Sandra to be more involved and advocate on my own behalf when physical illness struck. I learned to do what I preached for over thirty years. I learned to listen to my body.

After a lifetime of struggling to find a cure for Sandra's difficulties, I was left feeling that both bipolar disorder and schizophrenic tendences listed in the Diagnostic and Statistical Manual of Mental Disorders (DSM-5) may not be disorders at all but a genetic maladaptation which I explore in the last part of the book.

Change is needed now both for vulnerable people and for their care as society plans for future generations.

FINDING BALANCE

My journey began by trying to find psychological 'balance' for my sister Sandra. Oprah Winfrey continues to search for what she thinks she needs but did not get at an early age.[1] I searched with Sandra and ended up discovering that balance has many sides.

At age twenty, while living with our elderly parents, Sandra threw a chair through the bedroom window of a sixth-floor apartment. It took three burly police officers to restrain her and remove her from the home she had occupied for the previous ten years. She had incredible strength for a young woman of slight build.

I sat alone 100 km away wondering how I could help.

Should I advocate for Sandra? Should I advocate for our parents? I wanted to do the impossible and cure Sandra.

> "Start by doing what's necessary.
> Then do what's possible; and
> Suddenly you are doing the impossible."
>
> - Francis of Assisi

I knew that it was necessary to remove Sandra from the apartment and settle our parents. Heartbreak number one came when Sandra was admitted to the psychiatric wing of a nearby hospital.

---

[1] *People Magazine*, May 31, 2021

Six weeks later, at the last-minute, when Sandra was about to be discharged from the hospital, the answer to our prayers came in the form of an acceptance letter from the Canadian Army.

Over the next year, Sandra passed six weeks of basic training with flying colors. She trained in Ontario and spent time on both the east and west coasts of Canada. Sandra became a trained postal clerk. She looked fantastic: strong, fit, and beautiful.

Like a lightning bolt, word came from Montreal less than a year later that Sandra had received a medical discharge; the diagnosis was that she was suffering from schizophrenic tendencies. She was in jail and claiming that she was the Virgin Mary.

It was 1975, before Google, so I went back to the books. At that time, the medical stance was to 'blame the mother' for her child-rearing practices, as if our mom had caused Sandra's illness. They were wrong. We were a family of five children, Robert Marion, Joseph Victor, Charlotte Antonia, Christine Irene and Sandra Marion. Four of us had successful jobs, owned our own homes and raised eight grandchildren. Mom used the same child-rearing practices with all of us.

They said that Sandra was confused and disoriented, but they also flipped between a diagnosis of schizophrenia and manic depression, now called bipolar disorder.

Sandra and I communicated throughout that time and throughout her life. She sent me letters, post-cards, and limericks. She visited with me whenever she could. By this time, I had two children and lived a distance away with my husband and our little family. Sandra's words may have been out of context, and she may have struggled to find the right word, but by focusing and listening closely, I could always interpret what she was trying to say.

I smile at this last paragraph, because in a recent text to my sister-in-law Shirley, my phone did an auto correct. When I looked at the message. I immediately texted again and told her what I meant. I called the autocorrect feature 'stupid.' She said, "That's all right. I understand text talk." Similarly, I always understood someone trying to find the right word. That ability served me well in my later years when physical illness and medication caused me to struggle to find the right word. The challenge didn't scare me. It caused me to focus harder and find an alternate way to get my message across.

Sandra hated her medication. She went off it whenever she could. She took Tylenol 3, alcohol, and sometimes heavy drugs to try and self-medicate.

Because of the tendency at the time to look for what went wrong, traditional physicians looked for problems that may or may not have existed. Over the years, Sandra and I watched other family members struggle with similar issues.

With the diagnosis of mental illness in our family, you would think that our lives growing up must have been horrible. In fact, our brother Bob once commented that we would have been better off if we had been raised in an orphanage. I was shocked. Bob, a brilliant man in his own right, was diagnosed and treated for bipolar tendencies in his late forties. Sandra's life clearly was a nightmare, but I grew up in the same family, experienced the same environment, and somehow managed to live a life full of happiness, but not without pain; success, but not without work; and balance, with much effort.

I tackled 'the necessary' by getting Sandra out of our parents' apartment. Then I turned my attention to 'what's possible?' I wanted to find out why I seemed balanced, and some other members of our family struggled to find it. I spent the next 40 years believing that 'finding balance' was the key to our family's challenges.

Life is a great balancing act. Each aspect of our life is in some way a balance between two things. To achieve physical health, our body strives to maintain a balanced temperature, neither too hot nor too cold. Healthy weight is maintained by finding a balance between caloric intake and output. To achieve peace of mind we make a moral choice of choosing what is right and what we perceive may not be right. To find a complete system for total health, we also need to add a sense of calm and clarity, or mental balance.

It is the mental balance that has become our greatest challenge. We are no longer living in an age of information. We are living in an age of information overload.

Lao Tzu once said:

> "If you are depressed, you are living in the past
> If you are anxious, you are living in the future
> If you are at peace, you are living in the present."

The ideal state is one of living in the present, with just enough anxiety to be aware of any potential future danger and just enough memory not to repeat past mistakes, but also to explore and build on past learning and experiences. The key is to increase the amount of time you spend in the present and to explore the other two states of consciousness as cautionary aids to assist in navigating this ever-changing world.

Change is an inescapable part of life. Without change there is no growth, no movement, and no life. Dealing with change in our lives is both mentally and physically exhausting.

We need to learn to address and support changes that enable everyone to develop a lifestyle over which they can have direct control. It will not be the same lifestyle for all of us and we must learn to acknowledge and accept differences in preference and lifestyle.

Balance is a skill. With practice and patience anyone can learn a new skill. Our sense of balance may not be identical to the next person's. It is irrelevant how far we go in our search. The most important thing is that we reach a point with each action where we can learn and change. Life is change.

Michio Kaku, a prominent modern-day physicist, comments in one of his books, *Future of the Brain*, that movies really depict someone's thoughts on the future and much of what we thought was fantasy could eventually become reality. I remember watching STAR TREK as a child and thinking that it could never happen. It is happening. We are exploring space! There is a long running TV series called HOMELAND. The lead character played by Claire Danes is a CIA agent who suffers from bipolar tendencies, but she is really the 'best of the best' in terms of insight and creative thinking. She knows that she needs external supports to maintain her 'balance' and control her unbalanced tendencies. When she can control them, she achieves what many consider to be impossible.

In this book, I want the reader to look at all the things that went right in our family rather than focus only on what may or may not have gone wrong.

Chapters one through seven document our family's everyday lives and our mom's childrearing practices. I wrote with the intent that professionals working in this field of study would appreciate the normal lives we had as I share our perceptions and struggles. The reader will learn about how cumbersome the long-term care admission process continues to be and the changes required to support future unique generations. As we struggled to find that elusive balanced lifestyle, in considering both mental and physical changes in life, I discovered a unique epigenetic possibility that needs to be fully explored if humanity is to continue to evolve.

I moved toward that sought-after sense of balance with the hope of finding 'a cure' for Sandra. I may have been wearing rose-colored glasses throughout my life, but this is where my search for understanding began.

Chapter One

OUR EARLY YEARS (1945-1954)

I don't remember a lot from those years and sometimes memory is creative, but there are always several instances that pop into mind occasionally. Some are accurate memories and others are memories created from pictures we saw or stories we heard.

My earliest memory from those years comes from an experiment that I participated in when I attended a psychology class as an adult student. The focus was on repressed memories. Our professor had invited a guest speaker from California to attend our class. The man was a hypnotist as well as a psychologist. He relayed a story about a woman who had difficulty getting pregnant. She came to him for help. He hypnotized her and took her back to when she was in the birth canal. She heard her father shouting, "No, no. I don't want this." She came out of the session and relayed what she had heard. She was in tears. The therapist asked her to call her mom and discuss it. Her mother was in Europe at the time, but she called and relayed her experience.

The young woman opened the conversation with, "I know dad didn't want me."

Her mother reassured her that the words she heard were accurate, but her interpretation was wrong. Her dad did say those words, but he said them in the taxicab on the way to the hospital. He did not want her to be born in a taxi, but he wanted her and loved her every day of his life. Her father was now deceased. The young woman cried tears of joy and thanked her mom. Within four months she was pregnant with the first of their three children.

The guest psychologist then asked for a volunteer from the class. No one raised their hand. I was an adult student, so I was a little more worldly than most of my classmates and more willing to take a risk. I raised my hand, thinking that I could not be hypnotized because I had such a strong mind. Surprise! Surprise! I immediately went back to my highchair years. I was there with my dad who was dressed in a white sleeveless undershirt and plaid pants. He stood beside me with a spoon but rather than feed me, he kept trying to put it in my right hand. Again and again he put that spoon in my right hand as I reached for it with my left. After the session, I described my experience and was asked to call my mom for clarification. I called that evening, and my mom did indeed verify that the experience happened as I described. She said that they realized early that I was using my left hand instead of my right hand, and because they felt that the world favored right handedness, they wanted to change my preference.

I never appreciated the significance of their labor until I was much older. I was taking a drawing class as an adult. We were asked to draw with our right hand and then draw with our left hand. I discovered that I could draw equally well with both hands. I have since lost most of that ambidextrous ability.

In my family I was one of five children. I was the middle child between two older brothers and two younger sisters. There was another brother, Michael, who died of spinal meningitis six months before I was born (December 1944). He died at eighteen months of age. I never knew Michael, but our parents never forgot him.

As I moved from toddler to child, I developed a special bond with my two brothers Bob and Joey. Bob was 5 years older than me, and Joey was 3 years older than me. Our mom made my brothers take me everywhere. They became my world.

When I was four years of age, our parents took our little family to Buffalo, New York on the Fourth of July. That just happens to be my birthday. My dad told me that all the fireworks and celebrations were for me. I thought, "What wonderful people," and to this day I love Americans for their celebration of my birthday.

Bob and Joey fought ferociously with each other, and our dad punished them by making them sit in opposite corners of the room and hold a small stool over their heads for hours! I could only watch them being punished for so long and then I would cry, and my dad would release them.

Dad used the stool, but mom wielded the strap. It was brown leather, about three inches wide and it had a slit up the center. It hung in the pantry beside the kitchen sink and was meant for immediate punishment. Mom never said, "Wait till your father gets home." I never experienced either the stool or the strap. I was either 'so good' or crying so hard before the punishment could be meted out that mom and dad would start laughing and just verbally scold me.

Up until the time I was about four years of age, my hair was long. It fell to my waist and my mom braided it daily. One day she got a call from a neighbor down the street who asked how my hair was. My mom looked at me and said, "Fine." She saw two long braids resting on my back.

The neighbor said that the girls were playing barber and Charlotte (me) cut Cassie's bangs right to her scalp. My mom scolded me. I cried and nothing more was said. I had cut Cassie's bangs straight across and she partially cut into my thick braids. The braids held until the next morning when they were unwound. Mom watched as my beautiful hair fell to the floor.

Every time I got my hair cut, the boys were threatened with the strap. It was always cut the same, bangs and a blunt cut below my ears. We would come home from the barber, and I would look at my brothers. They would burst out laughing. I would cry and Mom would head to the pantry for the strap. It was a hard lesson, but I learned how friends, as well as family, can influence and alter your life.

During these years I received my first communion, and my brothers received their confirmation. It stands out in my mind because they could read, and I could not. I forced my mom, dad, whomever I could find to read the passages that had been assigned aloud repeatedly until I had them memorized. I learned how to memorize which served me well throughout my school years. Understanding eventually came, but I memorized everything I could to excel at school.

Only once in all those years did my brothers frighten me, but it was not intentional. They wanted to see a horror movie, and, of course, the only way that they could go to the show was to take me with them. They didn't share with our mom which movie they wanted to see, and after I saw a woman pull a basket out from under her bed with a human head in it, I balked at going to bed for weeks. After our parents learned the reason for my bedtime tears, the boys got the strap for taking me to a scary movie.

Our dad managed to afford to raise five children, have a stay-at-home wife (at that time few moms worked), and keep us all well fed, well-dressed, and, in my memory only, happy. We were the first house on the street to have a black and white TV, and every Christmas the entire living room floor was covered with presents that were just what each of us wanted. Dad managed by moving his family multiple times. He would buy an old house. Fix it up by making small repairs and applying fresh paint and wallpaper. The process is often called 'lip sticking' today. Our parents would then sell the house for a profit, buy another house, and repeat the process.

As an adult, I now watch our adult children struggle with moving and having their children change schools and make new friends. I always looked on moving as an adventure. A new school, new friends, and a chance to reinvent myself. My old clothes would be new to my current classmates! I have always managed to stay connected with the best of friends. Years later one of my friends would remark that I collected 'friends' like other people collect butterflies or hockey cards.

One of our moves found us living in the Beaches District of Toronto. We were walking along the boardwalk with a large group of friends when someone said, "Look at the baby swimming." It was my sister, Christine, lying face down in the water near the shore. Joey immediately sat down on the shore and started taking off his shoes and socks. Bob ran in fully clothed and picked her up. I loved both of my brothers, but for me, Bob was my Tarzan! For me, 'family' was everything.

The first disappointment I had to struggle with was when our mom left our dad and went to her sister Stella's house in another city. Our dad was a 'weekend alcoholic.' Monday to Friday he worked. On Saturday he drank, and on Sunday he sobered up, apologized, and went off to work again Monday morning. In hindsight now, as an adult, I understand why our mom left. But at the time, I never thought about why she left. I was only shocked that she left me! She took Christine and Sandra with her but left me with the boys and our dad. That is all I remember about the incident, not what my mom did, but how she made me feel. At this early age, I learned that I could survive someone leaving me. I hated it, but I could survive.

At five years of age, my dad took me to work on a Saturday. He made his living by painting and paperhanging, both commercially and residentially. He was finishing the interior of a downtown Toronto office in a huge commercial high rise. Because it was a Saturday, there were few people working. Dad was in his fifties at the time and two thirty-something executives in full three-piece suits stepped into the elevator with us. Dad was in his coveralls and the young suits asked him a few questions. He answered by saying, "Yes sir," and "No sir." I wondered why my dad was calling these young men 'sir.' He was older, and they should have been calling him 'sir.' I never considered that my dad felt inferior or less. I never considered that dress or outfit could have been a factor. I never forgot that I felt that the young men were disrespectful. I continue to believe that age and wisdom deserve respect.

Christine was born on May 23, 1950. I was five at the time and in my memory, I felt that it was my responsibility to look after my sister Christine when she was one and I was six. I remember putting her in a wagon and walking her around the block. It must have been a daily routine. She was just a baby. On one trip around, she fell out of the wagon onto the cement sidewalk. She cried and cried. I cried too. I thought that I had killed her. We circled the block three times that day. She fell asleep and we went home.

I never told my mom what happened. I never told Christine either. The one regret that I can remember is that I did not tell my mom that Christine fell out of the wagon on our walk, but 'walking' has stayed with me throughout my life to mentally sort out difficulties or problems. I still walk, but now with a 100 pound Doberman Pinscher.

Around the same time, I experienced a second memorable birthday. My dad took me to the doll section of Eaton's Department Store. There was a whole wall of dolls. I thought I was in a magic land. He said, "Pick one, whichever one you want." I thought, "Wow. I am special and lucky." I picked a chubby, fair-sized doll with blonde hair whose name was Buttercup. I had her for years and often thought of that day and how special my dad made me feel.

Sandra was born on September 16th, 1952. Even though I was seven years of age, I can't remember ever seeing my mother pregnant. One day our dad took our mom to the hospital and said that they were bringing home a new baby. Her name was Sandra Marion. I loved both of my sisters.

Some of the following comments are from my memory but most are from a box of notes, drawings, and limericks and pictures that Sandra shared with me over the years.

Sandra was a highly active baby. There was no walking her around the block in a wagon. She would have jumped out. She escaped from everything and everywhere and was always running away. She always said that she hated our dog Tippy. Tippy did have some German Shepherd in her but, she was just a mutt. Our mom would only let Sandra out if Tippy accompanied her. Tippy never allowed anyone to speak to Sandra. She would growl and show her teeth and make sure that Sandra returned home unharmed.

We first called Sandra 'Pretzel Bender' because she could bend and twist her body in weird and wonderful ways, allowing her to escape from her crib, her stroller, and the house. Her nickname was eventually shortened to Pretzel, a name she answered to for years.

By the time Sandra was two, we were living in the house we called home for the next twenty years. There was a laneway out the back where all the kids played. We all went out after supper, played hide-and-go-seek, and came home when the streetlights came on. We always had the hardest time finding Sandra when she hid.

It would be years later before I learned that my siblings didn't view our dad in the same supportive way. Sandra wrote about being a child and walking down the lane behind the house with our dad, and Dad letting go of her hand and running ahead. Sandra started to cry and ran after him and just as she raised her hand to put it back in his, Dad looked down at her and told her that he wouldn't be around forever. He was always telling all of us that he was not long for this earth.

On January 2, 1992, nine years after Dad died, Sandra wrote that she hated our father and that she was glad when he died.

My last 'early years' memory occurred when I would have been ten years of age. Christine was five and Sandra was three. Children often pretend that they are a nurse, a teacher, or Wonder Woman. My sisters will confirm that I always believed that deep down I was a 'fairy princess.' I would bring both Christine and Sandra into the living room and ask them to share their dreams and wishes with me so that I could try and make them come true.

The three of us were playing in the living room. I can only assume from what transpired that I was in my 'Fairy Princess' mode. The living room was small, and the entire back wall consisted of a central fireplace (non-functional), with two nine-foot wooden pillars framing a large mirror in the center. Suddenly, the structure started to fall away from the wall. I yelled at my sisters to run, and I ran toward the fireplace to hold it up until they could escape.

The huge structure took me down with it, and the mantel stopped about a quarter inch from my throat. Our mom was hysterical until I carefully maneuvered my way out so that I would not cut myself on the broken glass. I learned that if I relaxed and 'listened' to my body, I would know what to do. I was worried about my sisters. I was also shocked that I could not hold up that massive structure. To this day, I believe that I should have been able to hold that huge wooden structure in place.

Chapter Two

ROSE-COLORED GLASSES (1955-1964)

These were my 'wild years.' Most adults remember their university years as their most memorable years, but for me it was senior elementary and high school. From here on, all anecdotes are real memories. In school I was a mousey, quiet academic who would passionately argue a point, but who would never do anything wrong. I always remembered the strap!

At age eleven I went into a general store with my brother Joey. We walked around and looked at all the stuff. It was the year that Slinkys were popular. When Joey saw me playing with one, he asked if I would like it. I said yes but knew that neither of us had more than a quarter in our pockets. We continued to look around inside the store. Once outside the store, and on our way home, Joey pulled out the slinky and handed it to me. I almost died right there. He had stolen it! I looked at him, appalled. He laughed and walked over to the newspaper box and grabbed a bunch of change. At that time customers just threw their money on top of the papers. "C'mon," he said, "I'll buy you an ice cream." He laughed at me all the way home as I cried and licked my ice cream. I was sure that he was going to jail.

Whereas both of my brothers influenced my early years, Joey was the 'main man' at this time. I need to share here that our mom was so overwhelmed with five children that when Bob was six and ready for school (no kindergarten at that time), she dressed both boys the same (Joey was tall for a three-year-old) and Mom said that they were twins. They both started school at the same time. It is a key point, because Joey was always so much younger than the rest of his classmates, so he never learned how to socialize with his peers at school. When he was sixteen, he went into hairdressing. We always said that it was because our mom went grey early, and he wanted to make her look better or maybe it was because of my blunt haircut and tears, but I think he just found it was one of the easiest courses in a technical school. His grades were not good enough to get him into an academic school and there was no way he was going to a commercial high school. Nevertheless, he did have a creative side that allowed him to shine throughout his chosen profession. While studying, he had to practice. He wanted to practice on me! I never knew what I was going to look like, so I made him 'pay me' to do my hair every day before I went to high school. I looked like a model every day. He did fancy braiding, French twists, and knots on the top of my head. Some days I showed up as a blonde, some days a redhead, but mostly I was a brunette with blonde streaks, which were popular at the time. I can still hear Joey saying whenever he pulled my hair, "You have to suffer to be beautiful!" By the time I married at age twenty and moved away from home, my hair had grown back into its natural brunette color. My dad commented that he did not like that color on me! I was the only one out of his five children who had naturally brunette hair. The other four were all blonde.

During these years both Bob and Joey earned money. We had a small house, a television, and one chesterfield. Bob or Joey got the chesterfield because they would send either me or Christine to the corner store to buy treats for us all. That act of sharing guaranteed them a place of comfort. We sat on the floor and munched away on snacks watching the regular weekly series of Rin Tin Tin, Lassie, The Lone Ranger, and The Ed Sullivan Show.

Life was good. I excelled at school. We had the first television set on the street. Our brothers behaved well. Our mom cooked and cleaned and opened our house and table to all our friends. The exception was on weekends when Dad drank. He was mean, loud, verbally abusive, and extremely jealous.

Sandra wrote that our dad made her angry when he would say bad things about our mother. She was too young to do anything, but she hated him for his drunken comments.

In grade five I got 98 percent on a test. We always went home for lunch and so I shared my mark with my mom and returned to school. The teacher asked what my mother had said when she saw my mark. I said that she asked what question I had missed. My teacher repeated that comment numerous times throughout the year. I never understood why he was so impressed.

Mom was proud of my academic achievements and excused me from all kinds of work around the house. It made her happy, so I continued to study and memorize my way through school.

Years later, Sandra would comment in an undated remark that my siblings only argued about the fact that I was always excused from housework because I was the fairy princess.

Sandra struggled with school and broke her glasses regularly, which led to a disaster because she couldn't see anything without her glasses. She wore what we called coke bottle glasses. The lenses were made of very thick glass. They weighed heavily on her little face. She always wore her hair short and always wore shorts or long pants under her dresses. Sandra often pretended to be sick as an excuse to stay home from school. She shared with me that the biggest problem that she had experienced in grade school was when she went to beat up a girl and the girl told the teacher. She told me how the other kids teased her about being ugly and not being able to speak very well. Sandra had A lisp which we hardly noticed, and which she eventually outgrew. She wrote that she wanted to be an educated bum when she grew up.

Until I read her notes, I had never realized that Sandra had been bullied. She never shared those experiences and I never thought to probe. When she wrote about wanting to beat up a classmate who had been mean to her, I was not surprised to hear that Sandra fought.

Broken bones from falls were a regular occurrence with Sandra. She described herself as clumsy. She broke her ankles more than once when she jumped into cardboard boxes and fell coming down off a teeter totter. She broke her collarbone by falling backwards and her finger when she fell off a stool. It would be years before we discovered that she had extremely high arches and an uneven gait which made walking difficult and falling easy. This may or may not have been the reason for all the falls. She writes that she had "no fear; she was careless; a dumb child." Sandra describes pretending that she was dancing when she had a broken ankle. She came in and acted like nothing was wrong. She fell. Both Mom and Dad saw that her ankle was broken. They argued about who would have to take her to the hospital.

I remember bringing home a friend who had no lunch. Her name was Ella-Mae Ash, and she was black. I only mention it here because we never saw 'color' differences when we were growing up. Ella-Mae said that she lost her lunch, but she was also wearing just the lining of a coat. It was December and it was cold. I did not have to ask my mom whether she could stay for lunch. I just had to say that she had no lunch.

While my friend was eating, I asked my mom if she could find her a coat downstairs. My mom smiled and said, "My other children bring home dogs and cats, and you bring home needy children." She then said that she would have to call my friend's mother first and ask if it would be all right if she gave my friend an 'extra' coat that I had outgrown. I really did not outgrow it. Mom went to rummage sales, thrift, and consignment shops to find enough outfits to clothe her five children at a fraction of their original cost. She had a huge closet in the basement where she hung clothes that were in excellent condition and into which we would eventually grow. Before this day I never knew that it was possible for someone to decline food or a coat because of pride. Ella-Mae returned to school having eaten a hot lunch and wearing a colorful, warm coat.

Mom continued her bargain hunting even when we could afford to buy new. She loved the hunt. Today her activities would be referred to as a 'side hustle.' She had an eye for good clothing. She would pay a pittance, bring them home, wash and iron them, and take them to a consignment store for resale. She was a woman before her time.

Because I had grown-up with my brothers watching over me, I knew all their friends and they all knew me. It didn't seem odd that I would hang around with an older crowd. Joey did not really feel comfortable with his classmates who were all older than him, so he became the ultimate 'big brother.'

As I mentioned earlier, Joey became an exceptionally good hairdresser. One of his clients was hosting Princess Margaret, the Queen's sister, on a visit to Canada. She asked if Joseph would come to her condominium and do Princess Margaret's hair. He was sixteen years old and too nervous so he declined, but it gives you an idea of how talented he was.

At 18 years of age, he was working full time and making more money than our dad ever made. He got his driver's license and bought himself a baby blue Pontiac Parisienne convertible. Where did he go to show off? He picked me up after my shift at Woolworth's and drove me home. All the other salespeople ogled and awed at both the car and the driver. Of course, I never let on that he was my brother.

Joey asked if he could go with me to pick out a dress for my first high school dance. No one went as a couple in those days. We just went in groups. I knew that Joey was much worldlier than I was when it came to fashion, so I let him choose which dresses I should try on. He brought several to the changing room door. I tried them on and modelled for him. We narrowed it down to two dresses: a large floral print that fell in folds from the waist to just above the knee and a black fitted dress that was a little shorter. We could not decide. I had saved enough money to purchase one of the dresses. I asked him to choose. I changed into my street clothes and walked out of the dressing room. He handed me a designer bag with both dresses in it. He told me to use my money for shoes. Joey, of course, did my hair.

Later that same summer, one cousin named June came from St. Catharines for a holiday. June was two years younger than me and five inches taller than my five-foot-seven-inch height! She stood six-foot two inches tall. Joey was also six foot two inches tall. The three of us had a blast. We went to the zoo, in Joey's convertible, of course. We went to the Toronto Exhibition, Algonquin Park, and Ottawa so he could give his car a good run. Joey paid for everything. I did not ask or request, but I also did not say 'thank you' enough.

Joey eventually met and married a Macedonian woman named Helen from his hairdressing class. Joey now wanted to be called Joseph, but at home we still called him Joey. I thought Helen was very sophisticated and knew everything. She arranged classy dinners, threw amazing parties, and taught proper etiquette to those of us who wanted to learn. Through Helen's church, I attended dances, dinners, and unique events with her and Joey.

One Halloween, Helen went to her church dance dressed as an artist. Joey dressed as a lady of the night, wearing a red wig, a slinky black dress, four-inch heels, and the legs to pull it all off. He walked better in those heels than I ever could. No one knew who he was. My hair was blonde at the time, and Joey added a long, blonde ponytail. I dressed as a biker chick with black leather pants and jacket. We had a lot of fun until several of the male attendees started hitting on me. Remember, I was only sixteen, and they were in their early twenties. Joey was furious and immediately put them in their place. It looked funny to see him threatening the guys while in his dress and heels, but he was quite a large figure to begin with being six foot two inches tall in bare feet and then wearing four-inch spikes. At the time I was annoyed with his interference, but now I look back with fondness on my big brother looking after me.

I met my lifelong friend in grade nine. Mary was always taking notes. I knew that she was listening, but she still wanted to make notes. Most teachers put up with her idiosyncrasy, but one became downright nasty. Our history teacher wanted everyone to listen to him and make notes afterwards. This teacher started yelling and slammed his ruler on her desk. Mary didn't get upset but yelling and any hint of punishment affected me negatively. I felt so sorry for her. We went to our French class next, and when Mary started taking notes I leaned forward and said that I had a good memory, and I would give her the notes I had made after class. I thought, poor Mary, she must need extra help to excel. At the end of term, I advanced with an acceptable 80+ average. Mary came in at 98 percent! Mary was my maid of honor at my first wedding and to this day remains my best friend.

In grade eleven, I tried out for the trampoline club. I didn't make it. I was incredibly angry because I really liked it and I knew that if I practiced, I could improve. That summer I took my regular trek to St. Catharines to stay with my Aunt Stella, Uncle John, and cousin June. Mom thought that she was doing me a huge favor by getting me out of the city (of Toronto) for a few weeks. She would have had me stay for a month, but I always wanted to come home.

Aunt Stella and Uncle John lived on a fruit farm with their two daughters. Betty, the eldest, suffered from Down's Syndrome and my Aunt Stella devoted her entire life to her daughter's care.

Aunt Stella ran their fruit farm. Uncle John worked at the dry docks. They requested that I come every year as a playmate/companion for June, their youngest daughter. I was told that I could earn money by picking fruit. I was OK with the plums, pears, and cherries, but I hated even walking into the peach orchard where there was a feeling of fuzz hanging thick in the hot and humid air. It made my skin crawl.

Within walking distance of my aunt's farm was a beach with a carnival called Port Dalhousie. They had a merry-go-round, some games, a few rides, and a trampoline activity center. It cost a quarter for 15 minutes, but because so few children took advantage of the trampoline, the owners would let me jump and jump to demonstrate what people could do on a trampoline. I spent every waking hour when I wasn't picking fruit, practicing. By the end of my visit, I could do front flips, back flips, seat to belly turns and numerous other antics. I returned to school that fall, demonstrated my ability in a regular gym class, and smiled as I walked away from the awe-struck trampoline team.

Both Sandra and Christine spent time at our Aunt Stella's farm when they were young. We all had fond memories of life on a fruit farm but all of us preferred life in the city.

That same year, a small group of my high school classmates and I decided to support a candidate for school president. In our eyes, and I should add also in his, Mike was the most unlikely candidate for school president that you would ever want to meet. We were all doing it as a lark, and also because we wanted to have campaign parties and fun. We made posters and pamphlets, and early one morning before we left on a class trip, we hung a huge banner right across the front of the school. The banner was removed by the time we got back, and we all had a good laugh. The next day all candidate speeches took place. I have never forgotten how shocked I was when our candidate stepped up to the podium in a suit and tie and presented a much-rehearsed speech geared to win over voters. Somewhere along the way, Mike had crossed the line from fun to serious and he really wanted to win. He didn't win, but it became a life lesson for me. If you think you can, maybe you can.

The summer I turned 17, Sandra was ten. I had a goal of dating all the lifeguards along Toronto's boardwalk. They were fit and good-looking, and dating sites weren't invented yet. I started at Greenwood Pool and went out with two of the lifeguards there. One was in my grade, but the other was a little older and had to return to Germany to put in his two years in the Army. While away, he wrote to me. Being polite I wrote back but was not overly affectionate. I stopped writing when I received a marriage proposal in the mail!

Sandra noted that I would take her to the pool with me. She could swim underwater but not on top. She wondered if she would ever learn to swim on top but at the end of one summer season, she did learn. She was disgusted when all the lifeguards started hitting on me. She made a point of noting that I always had boyfriends and that she would just tag along.

Only one of my lifeguard dates proved embarrassing. Lifeguard number three and I were walking down Yonge Street on a Saturday evening. We were cruising arm in arm down Yonge Street when a drunken person came up behind us and put his hand on my shoulder. My companion had him up against a plate glass window in a flash. I had to ask him to release the person because the drunk was my dad. It was Saturday evening, Dad's night to drink. Both men were shocked at my words. My date released my dad and we continued with our evening. My dad never mentioned the incident and neither did I.

Sandra started smoking and drinking around ten years of age. She'd steal cigarettes and sneak into dad's stash of rye whenever an opportunity arose. I never saw or heard anything about her escapades, but my mind was on other things.

There were seven of us living in the house. Five family members smoked. Most were two pack-a-day smokers. Neither my mom nor I smoked.

Our mom and dad often found Sandra's hidden stash of alcohol and cigarettes. She wrote about mom punishing her with the strap. Both Sandra and Bob lied and ran away from home. Sandra writes that she took after our brother Bob, and that they got the most lickings. They were disciplined and it hurt me to watch, but it made sense to me that their actions should be corrected.

She didn't watch much TV as a child, but she read *Old Yeller*, *Savage Sam*, and *Huckleberry Finn*.

I found her notes where she commented that she fell in love with Keir Dullea, the star of David and Lisa, a popular movie about a group of psychiatric patients. She wondered if it was a sign of how sick she was.

If our family had known that Sandra had concerns about her behaviors, we may have been able to initiate some help early on, but we never saw anything wrong and mental illness was a foreign concept to us. We all went on with our busy, separate lives. No one ever saw anything 'wrong' with Sandra. She went to school. She had a circle of friends, and she loved her family. She struggled at school and even though she shared that she smoked and drank alcohol, I never saw any of it. I wonder if I really did wear rose-colored glasses.

I continued to excel at high school. Three different teachers told my mom that I should go to university. No one in our family had ever gone to university and she would have done anything to have made that happen.

In grade ten I had a young English teacher, David B. Our class was his first teaching assignment after graduation. He was impressed with the way I thought and expressed myself. I was dating a fellow student at the time, having given up on lifeguards. Mr. B. had obviously purchased season tickets at the Royal Alexandra Theater in Downtown Toronto. Whenever he couldn't go, he passed the tickets along to us, introducing us to live theater.

My most embarrassing high school moment occurred in Mr. B.'s class. We had physical education right before his class and there was never enough time to change and run to class. I was never shy about undressing in gym class. When most girls went behind curtains to change, I just grabbed my clothes, found a bench, stripped, and dressed. One day we were running late. I went into change mode and put on my slip and dress which had buttons from top to bottom (in the front). I ran up to class taking two steps at a time and took my front row seat right in front of Mr. B's desk ready for the class lesson. I watched as his face turned from white to pink to red to a deeper red before I looked down and realized that not one button on my dress was fastened. The dress had opened down the center when I sat down and there I was in front of our young, good-looking English teacher sitting in my slip, which was underneath my dress. I looked down and immediately started to close the buttons as Mr. B. moved to the far side of the classroom to conduct the class.

Throughout my high school years, I met and dated many young men. I looked good with a personal hairdresser and two brothers who spoiled my every whim. I also knew who I could run to for help or protection if I found myself in an uncomfortable situation. In my early years, our dad was an extremely strict disciplinarian. Dad was getting older, smaller, and weaker. My brothers were getting older, bigger, and stronger. Dad would tell me when I went out that I had to be home by nine. If I wasn't home at nine, I would find the front door locked. As children and even young adults living in our parents' home, none of us ever had a key. I would have to knock, and wake up my dad so that he would know what time I got home. My wonderful brothers would take turns and wait up to let me in whenever I was out on a date and returning after nine.

By this time, I had met a classmate who wasn't a lifeguard but who was as smitten with me as I was with him. Right after we graduated from grade thirteen, Herb and I were married in a small church across from our high school and had a wedding celebration in my parents' home.

I was expecting our first baby at the time. My best friend Mary and one of Herb's sisters, Shirley, were my bridesmaids. They still laugh about the fact that they bought more beautiful dresses than I had for the wedding. I wore the same dress that I had worn as bridesmaid for my brother Joe's wedding three months prior. They did look amazing. I just wanted to get the wedding over and to get on with our lives. Christine and Sandra should have been my bridesmaids. I was embarrassed that I had to rush to get married. I know that my mom was disappointed with my pregnancy, but fortunately she lived long enough to see me graduate with a master's degree in Community Psychology as an adult student. Joe and Helen had a huge fairy tale wedding three months prior. They were married in a large church and had an elaborate wedding reception in the Seaway Towers in Toronto. It had been expensive for our family. I didn't want my mom to have to put out more money for dresses for Christine and Sandra. I recently shared this regret with Christine who said that she was glad that I didn't ask her to be a bridesmaid because she just wanted to get back from the church and get drunk!

Christine was fifteen and Sandra was thirteen when I married and moved away. None of us noticed anything odd or different in how Sandra behaved or how she perceived the world. She was funny and would make us laugh all the time. I just remember that she hid on the roof and wouldn't say good-bye to me.

Christine and Sandra wore the same dresses to my wedding that they had worn to Joe and Helen's wedding. Mom wore the same dress as well, but she had it shortened to hang just below her knees. I never realized at the time that our mother was an incredibly beautiful woman. Even after having six children, mom still had a trim, girlish figure. She was five foot eight and had fantastic legs and a smile that would light up a room. Our Aunt Stella shared with me that when our mom and she would walk down the street, even though our mom was pushing a baby carriage, all eyes turned to look at our mom. It's important to note here that my Aunt Stella was six foot one and had been first runner-up in a Miss Toronto Contest as a teenager. She was a beautiful woman as well.

Our mom really was a woman before her time. She raised six children. One brother I never met, Michael, died at 18 months of age from spinal meningitis.

Mom was two months pregnant with me when her baby boy died. She cooked. She cleaned. She managed to provide us with everything we needed on a minimal allowance from our dad. She never complained, never verbalized that she wanted more. Our house had an open-door policy.

At fifty years of age, she went out and got a job working in the dietary department of a local hospital. That was 'her turn.' She excelled at her work and was asked to move into management. She declined. Mom became a shop steward and took employee grievances to local union meetings. I watched this housewife turn into a force to be reckoned with. She never shirked her duties at home and, as I previously mentioned, I am ashamed to admit that I never thought of offering to help. She got up at 4 in the morning and took public transportation to be at work by 6:00 A.M. She was home at 3 in the afternoon and made meals for our dad and for us. She saved and saved and was very generous in helping her children whenever they needed help. I watched this transformation from my late teens on and I thought that I also could be more. I wanted our children to strive to be the best they could be and never settle for 'good enough.'

Chapter Three

THIS WAS US (AGE 20 TO 30) 1965-1974

Herb and I had a beautiful baby girl 6 months after we married. Lisa was born on February 21, 1966, at Women's College Hospital in Toronto. Christine was sixteen. Sandra was fourteen. I had gained twelve pounds, and few people knew that I was pregnant.

I was thrilled but also very, very scared. No one really taught me how to raise a baby, let alone run a house or even cook! I had been spoiled. My mom excused me from household chores so that I could study. What did I do to thank her? Got pregnant, got married, and thought poorly of her because she wasn't excited for me. These were the years that I gave up myself, hence the altered chapter title from the current popular TV show "This Is Us." I had a romantic vision, as do many young women, that I would get married, have children, and live happily ever after.

I suffered from an acute urinary tract infection (UTI) throughout my first pregnancy. My routine checks were followed at the UTI clinic in the hospital rather than obstetrics. I was prescribed a sulphur-based medication that I took for the final four months of my pregnancy.

To prevent another unplanned pregnancy, I chose to have an Intra-uterine Device (IUD) inserted. The next thing I knew, I was back at Women's College Hospital, having my picture taken for an upcoming magazine article, praising this new direction in preventing unwanted pregnancies. I was one of the first failures. I was pregnant again! Like my mom, I didn't put on much weight, and at 8 months pregnant, I could still work as a receptionist.

Mom did everything for our dad and for us. I never even knew that she could read until she was in her fifties and had moved into a two-bedroom apartment with our dad and Sandra. When I commented, she said that she just never had the time. She was my role model along with Herb's mom, Cornelia (Cor), who had raised her children as a single mom and who was closer to them than anyone I had ever met. Cor invited the three of us- Herb, me, and baby Lisa- to move in with them while I worked, and Herb went to Teacher's College. Cor would look after Lisa and her grandson Glenn who she later adopted. She cooked and cleaned and looked after the babies. I wasn't any more help to my mother-in-law than I was to my own mom, and as soon as Herb graduated, I wanted to move away. I did not want Cor to take (and adopt) our baby as well.

Herb and I had an agreement. While he attended Teacher's College, I would go to work. He knew that I wanted to go to university, and we agreed that when he had completed his education it would be my turn. In those days (1960s) teachers were so much in demand that an individual could go to Teacher's College for nine months and immediately get a teaching job.

We were poor but happy and we loved each other. We rented an apartment in the beaches section of Toronto. Six weeks after Lisa was born, I went to work as a receptionist and Herb applied to Teacher's College.

I was so proud of my daughter's beautiful face, dark blue eyes, and bald head. I knew that she would be blonde. Years 1-3 went as planned. Our son Brett, baby number two, arrived fourteen months after Lisa. Brett was big. Lisa was petite. Even though they were fourteen months apart many people thought that they were twins. She was bald for a few years after Brett was born so I taped little bows to her head so that everyone would know that she was a girl.

Herb applied and was successful in securing a teaching position in what I considered the far north. It wasn't by today's standards, but I grew up in downtown Toronto. My parents never drove a car, and I had my brothers and street cars. I never had any desire to learn to drive. With the help of my husband's generous Uncle Charlie, we were able to buy a manse (house that had belonged to a church) in Holstein, Ontario. By my parents' standards, it was huge. It even had a set of back stairs for the serving staff.

In May 1969, Christine gave birth to her beautiful baby daughter Candy two weeks before her nineteenth birthday. There were babies everywhere. Bob and Shirley had baby Nicole, and Joe and Helen adopted Michael. Sandra was in her glory being an aunt. Our mom took everything in stride.

I was content to raise our little family and work when I could. My 'turn' was further delayed when Herb came home and announced that his salary would increase with each university credit he received (teachers needed fifteen credits to graduate). It made sense that I continue to work until he completed his degree.

When Sandra was fifteen, my husband, two babies, and I moved 200 km away where Herb had secured a teaching job. His uncle helped us with the purchase of a house. And since I was no longer within driving distance, could not drive, and had two small children, Sandra and I communicated by mail and Sunday night phone calls. Sandra was not exhibiting any signs of a struggle with balance and mental illness was still a hush, hush term.

There I was with two babies, no car, and stuck out in the middle of no-where. I walked two miles every day with those babies. A mile to the local country store and a mile back. I had a wagon in the summer and a sleigh in the winter as I patiently waited for my turn. I invited the local ladies in to quilt in our dining room. I was the only one in the community who had a room with no furniture where we could set up a quilting frame and leave it from week to week. I learned to quilt. Neighbors invited me into their homes for tea. They talked about the weather, the crops, and their kids. I talked about my kids, didn't care about the weather, and, to this day, can't tell you the dif-ference between grain or wheat.

Four years later found me pregnant again with our youngest daughter Lori. By the time I was seven months pregnant, I was bored out of my mind. Lisa and Brett were in school, and I was home alone. I looked around and saw that our barn needed painting. I grabbed the can of paint we had chosen and climbed up an extension ladder to paint the top boards of the barn. The neigh-boring farmers complained to Herb that they had to come in from the fields, because they couldn't stand to see a seven-month pregnant woman up a ladder painting. Little did they know that my dad worked on a swing stage painting tall buildings so that height and paint were familiar and comfortable for me.

Along came our last bundle of joy. We had three gorgeous children, all blonde with blue eyes, a bright beautiful girl, a handsome little man, and a beautiful feisty daughter. My husband was a teacher, and everyone thought that I should be happy and satisfied. I wanted more. I wanted 'my turn.' By this time, I had worked three successful jobs in the community after securing my driver's license. The area was so remote that the driving tester taught me to parallel park before he approved my license. My first job was with Werby Industries, a division of MacTac. I was hired as a clerk, but since good help was hard to find in a small community, I filled in for every opportunity that arose in the plant and soon knew all positions. I learned all the accounting skills that would serve me well in my future professional and personal life. The only negative side to this position was the life of the accountant and his wife. His wife and I had become good friends, and while my supervisor was a wonderful man at work, he was an abusive husband at home. After he had roughed her up one too many times, I physically helped her and their three children move into a home of their own. The General Manager of Werby Industries loved Little Theater and he was anxious to start one in Mount Forest. He asked me to audition for various parts. He was an artistic director as well as an outstanding actor. I auditioned and acted in his plays for three years. Memory work came easily for me so moving in and out of character became fun and took my mind off 'my turn.' The camaraderie of working with a cast of people was exhilarating and I loved when other actors forgot their lines and we would have to improvise to cover up and move forward so that the audience would not realize that a mistake had been made. We did a lot of Neil Simon plays, and I always seemed to get typecast as a dumb blonde. I wasn't even blonde. I was brunette with blonde streaks. However, we were living in a small town so when I met people on the street, they thought that I had the characteristics of the character that I was portraying.

My final position before Lori's birth was with the Ontario Provincial Police (OPP). They created a front desk receptionist position because senior staff felt that constables were being paid too much money to sit at a desk all day. The sad thing was that when they created the position, it came without a job description other than 'transfer calls when they come in.' The calls that came in were rare because we were a district office, not a local office. Walk-ins were even fewer because the OPP building was in the country.

I answered the phone when it rang and directed the calls. I also memorized the Record, now called the Waterloo Region Record (newspaper) daily. One Monday I came in to work to find my desk drawers taped shut. When I removed the tape, I found every article inside — pencils, pens, sharpeners, paper clip box — taped down. Obviously, my position was not the only one that lacked stimulation. Even though the hours were fewer and the pay was more, I was grateful when my third pregnancy allowed me to gracefully bow out after six months of employment.

I eagerly reviewed the courses being offered on extension each semester. My husband still had three courses to complete, but my time was coming closer. He disliked university and he couldn't wait to finish. I can honestly say that if I had hated university work or did poorly, we might still be married today. He is a good man, and, in his own way, he loved me and our children. When he would come home from teaching school at age 23 or 24 and say, "Charlotte, I deal with kids all day at school. I don't want to deal with kids when I get home," it made sense to me. We were close in age. I was a year older than him.

Like all moms, I wanted to expose our children to as many opportunities as possible. Funds were limited but we were both working so there was enough money to have some extras. I also inherited some of my mom's financial skills and became creative with extras. I planned simple birthday parties for our children that cost next to nothing (hot dogs, juice, and cake), made loot bags, and invested hours developing age-appropriate games. They followed treasure maps and had memory games and three-legged races. I worked hard to ensure that everyone had fun. More children than I could accommodate always wanted to be invited to birthday parties at our house.

Sandra struggled by herself for many years, but it wasn't until she was in her early twenties that we started to notice some unusual behaviors. She would laugh inappropriately and talk to no one that we could see. She shared that a man with a white beard came and sat at the foot of her bed some nights. She wrote to Pierre Trudeau on a regular basis. We wondered if her behavior was alcohol induced or if the use of drugs had caused her irrational actions.

We did act once we realized something was not quite right in Sandra's world. Sandra shared that the psychiatrists she saw asked her to speak with doctors and nurses training in the field of psychiatry, because she was so knowledgeable and could speak fluently about both her problems and her symptoms. Medical diagnoses flipped between issues dealing with schizophrenic tendencies and issues dealing with bipolar symptoms.

Other family members crossing three generations have been diagnosed with bipolar symptoms, leading me to think that the bipolar diagnosis may have been the correct one.

Sandra started to call and visit more frequently, sharing her fears, thoughts, and concerns. About that time, the direction that Herb and I created for our lives started to diverge. Herb and I no longer had a common vision. He wanted to teach and become a hobby farmer. I wanted to go to university, become a doctor, and cure Sandra

This was my life before my turn arrived.

MY TURN (AGE 30-39) 1975-1984

This decade really started when I was twenty-nine. Sandra was diagnosed as suffering from schizophrenia at 22 years of age. By this time, I had three children who were ages 8, 7 and 2.

I considered myself 'happy.' Not totally self-fulfilled because I still hadn't started university. I knew that my turn to go to university was coming and my goal was to 'cure' Sandra. I had worked for a family doctor for 8 years and felt that I could be a doctor and then go on to become a psychiatrist. I had a goal, a direction, and, I thought, the smarts to pull it off.

Whenever Sandra was in an agitated mental state, she would find me and ask, "Do I need to go in?" (a psychiatric hospital, as it was called in those days). Once, early in her diagnosis, she came to Holstein, the small community where my family lived. At the time, I thought that my husband was afraid of her.

Sandra loved dogs and everyone in the family always had at least one. She wrote about a time when she was visiting me in the country and wanted to walk a dirt road to the local store. A storm was forecast, and I insisted that she take the dog with her. When the storm picked up, she couldn't see the walking path and credits the dog with saving her life after he led her safely home. Years later when I visited Sandra at Bendale Acres, I would bring our Doberman who sat quietly by her side and let her run her fingers through his fur. She was the envy of all the residents who watched. I walked him around and let others have a turn, but Sandra got the most attention.

Sandra was shaking and scared. She talked to herself and laughed inappropriately. In hindsight, my husband may have been afraid for our children rather than himself.

Sandra was worried about going into a dark place and never coming back out. I thought about everything that I had. I thought about how little she had. I decided that if I could, I would accompany her into her dark place to try and understand. She came into my bedroom one night when I was sleeping. She stood by my bed until my eyes opened. Perhaps I was dreaming, perhaps not. The vision I saw was Sandra at five years of age. In reality, she was a woman in her early twenties. I asked her to wait, again perhaps just in my mind or in a dream. I vividly remember going into each of our children's bedrooms and kissing them good-bye. I thought that I may never see them again, but I had this burning desire to understand and to help if I could. I returned to meet Sandra.

As if she were a child, I took Sandra's little hand in mine and let her lead me into her fearful world. Even today, over 50 years later, the best way I can describe our journey is walking the 23rd psalm, "Yea though I walk through the valley of the shadow of death," (how Sandra felt) "I will fear no evil" (how I felt). Her dark place was full of death. I wondered why movies and stories only depict the dark, evil side of the unknown. I wondered if her understanding of death played any part in her inability to find balance.

I was not ready to admit to the world the area that I wanted to investigate was death and mental illness in hopes of finding balance for Sandra. I also wasn't ready to give up my quest. A few months later when our youngest daughter Lori came to me (at 4 years of age) and asked with tears in her eyes if it were true that I was a year older than her father, I smiled and said yes. Her tears became sobs as she bolted from the room. I failed to grasp the importance of the incident and tried to comfort her by making light of the matter. Lori was not to be consoled. For the next year she told everyone we met that I was a year older than her dad. At one point she refused to go to nursery school because they did not believe her. I had to go in and confirm that I was indeed a year older than my husband. Besides being confused, I was a little embarrassed at having to reveal this fact to whomever Lori deemed important.

The next occasion occurred when Lori was six. It enabled me to make sense out of her obsession with my age. I was reading Elisabeth Kubler-Ross and the stages of dying. As a spontaneous question, I asked Lori if she had ever worried about death. She sat calmly staring out the window and said, "No. But I know that you are going to die first because you are the oldest, and I am going to die last." I was shocked. I can't even remember what my initial reply was. Lori came back with, "Why do people have to die?"

I tried to compose my thoughts because at this point, I was aware of the importance of our conversation. I said something to the effect that when people grow old, they become tired and because they have seen everything, they are not unhappy to die.

Lori came back almost attacking me with her words, "What about Betty's children (Lori's babysitter), they died when they were babies. They didn't have time to see anything. Why did they have to die?"

I started to read more on the subject and learned that often children do equate death with being old. I wondered if this association was encouraged in our society. I even chose an old person to explain death to Lori.

Sandra and our family had recently lost our maternal grandfather.

I wondered how many aspects of death children developed by themselves and whether there were any consequences of being arrested in an early stage of understanding such that the sequence of stages essential to establishing a healthy attitude toward death is never complete.

I worked from Monday to Friday in a doctor's office in Mount Forest and drove an hour to Wilfrid Laurier University every Saturday to take university courses on extension. I was thrilled. I took two courses at a time: one in the morning and one in the afternoon. I can't even remember what my first two courses were, but my third course was Research Methods. We had to design a piece of research. I was hot and heavy into my quest to find a cure for Sandra. This was the beginning of my search for balance. I felt at that time that an incomplete death concept could have caused schizophrenia. I never did accept the fact that it was related to child-rearing practices and that our mom was somehow at fault. I designed a piece of research looking at children's views of death. The professor gave me a good mark, but I could tell that he had photocopied my submission because the staples had been moved. I was an adult student in my early thirties by this time. I felt confident enough to go up after class and tell him that I intended to run this proposal as my undergraduate thesis after I had completed the fifteen courses required to graduate. He said, "Why wait?"

Whether it was my age or one of my theatrical characters boldly speaking, I don't know.

I said, "Cut the red tape and I'll do it now."

The next week I was in a thesis writing class with six other students who had all completed their undergraduate degree. Cam McRae led the class, and because I was starting late, he kindly asked everyone to share their projects with me. I knew that they were speaking English because I heard the occasional "the" and "and," but I understood little else. I had completed two courses. They had completed fifteen. They spoke mathematical jargon and to this day multiple regressions, a statistical technique used to validate data, still baffles me.

My research focused on the fears and anxieties that may exist when personal loss has not been experienced. I learned that all children, whether they have experienced death or not, ask questions that hold meaning for them. Children are not fools. They soon wonder about death being the gate to a better life when they see so few people wanting to open it (Mitchell, 1977).

Children participating in the study were asked to pick up a paper cut-out of a male or female photograph (young, middle aged, or old) and show what they think happens when a person dies. I was more interested in who they chose than what they did with the cut-out. I thought that they would choose the old people. In this study, the children's choices were not affected by their personal experience with death or by the age of the deceased person they had known.

The background research is quite old now, but at the time, numerous studies linked subsequent depression, mental illness, and suicide with concerns about death. In 1944, Blum and Rosenzweig found that 39 percent of their 356 male schizophrenic subjects had experienced a sibling death and that most of these deaths had occurred before the patient was six years old. The results supported the possibility that the traumatic death of a family member may be a contributing factor to adult schizophrenia. However, subsequent research by Munro and Griffiths (1969) and Granville-Grossman (1966) failed to support this notion, and to date, no 'critical period' for death experience leading to psychological disorder has been confirmed.

The death of someone close has been associated with nightmares in childhood, delinquency in adolescence, and mental illness in adults. The fears and anxieties from a childhood loss may, for some, be a crippling experience leaving a lifetime of psychological scars.

The research was completed after two university credits but not presented as my undergraduate thesis until I had completed my fifteen credits.

In 1985 the Jean Piaget Archive Foundation from the University of Geneva requested a copy of my thesis to be indexed and included in their next annual catalogue.

The envelope was addressed to Dr. C.A. Gibson, which made me smile.

Fast forward a few years and with seven courses to my credit, I ventured into Research Methods II.

I had a knack for developing proposals. I was still on my journey to find balance for Sandra but every once in a while, I had to 'back off' and make sure that I still had my own. I vacillated between focusing on balance and gaining credibility so people would listen to what I presented. Research Methods II required us to design and run three small pieces of research. The course mark would be based on the highest two of the three marks. I received 38/40 for the first piece of research and 39/40 for the second. I spoke with our professor and said that I was satisfied with those marks and did not really want to run a third piece of research. He said that I had to complete three research studies or he would give me a zero. I decided to have some fun with my final requirement. My research question was, "What is the motivation for women to go to male strip clubs?" I asked the professor if he would allow me to run this research and he said only if he could tag along.

You need to know that this was the late 1970s and male strip clubs were a novelty. The women who attended went 'wild.' Most of them filled out the questionnaire and said that 'fun' was their key motivator, but there were many men who also attended. They also wanted to fill out the questionnaire. My initial intention was to throw out their responses until I started to read them. Spare none, they used different language, but they all said, "We always come alone, but we never leave alone."

I absolutely loved learning and several of my other courses influenced my thinking and my life. By other courses, I am referring to ones that were not focused on psychology. At the time I could not see their relevance, but years later, bits and pieces would come into play and affect both my direction and my life.

I really wanted to take Abnormal Psychology, but the class was full. I could only attend university on Saturdays because I worked Monday to Friday and had a family who needed their fair share of attention. I did not have the luxury of looking to see what other time specific courses were offered.

I spoke with the professor who taught Abnormal Psychology and said, "If I don't take this class, all that's available that fits into my schedule is a drawing course in fine arts."

"Great!" he shouted. "That is exactly what you need. You need to be more rounded, not just psychology, psychology, psychology."

I signed up for the drawing course because it fit in with my available schedule. The first morning of class, I watched as all my classmates walked in with their little suitcases filled with paint tubes.

At the end of class, I asked the professor what kind of class this was, and she said, "Painting 301."

I said that I thought it was a drawing course. She informed me that drawing was offered on Thursday evenings, and I still had time to switch. I could not attend Thursday evenings, so I purchased a set of brushes and a few tubes of paint and brought them to class in a plastic grocery bag. I was not going to invest hundreds of dollars in supplies when this was just an elective, or, as I described it, a 'filler' course.

We did a little drawing as we sketched our topic before we applied the color. My subject was two butterflies that crossed paths as they were changing direction. The 'path' took on the colors of each of the butterflies and created a mosaic of its own. The professor looked at my work and asked where I had learned to blend and match colors. I said that I didn't know. She commented that the most experienced artists would never try and create a work using the colors that she saw in my work. I was so proud. I rushed home and even though I was 38 years of age, I called my mom to share my professor's praise.

She said, "You do know that your dad was an artist, don't you?" Up until that moment, I had not known. But if I rewind my story, there were several hints. Our dad was a painter and decorator. I could draw equally as well with both hands; I painted the second story of our barn as a comfort activity. My mom went on to say that my dad had wanted to be an artist, but everyone told him that he couldn't support a family by selling paintings, so he chose a career that paid him a salary and allowed him to work in the medium he loved best.

I took a genetics course next but hated working with fruit flies. Nevertheless, a seed had been planted and I became much more sensitive to the whole realm of heredity, genetics, and evolution.

The other elective that I found interesting but unrelated to my field of study was geography. It was another course that fit in with an available time slot. It would be years before I applied the concepts that I had learned in that class to influence our future buying and selling of real estate and their locations to make the best possible return on our investments. Around this time, a few professors started talking to me about entering the master's program. One of my professors pulled me aside one day and asked if I ever felt like I was a fake. I immediately answered, "Yes." He smiled and said that he had just read an article that identified the fact that most successful people do think that they are fakes.

Life was good. Just as I was about to graduate, two professors approached me and insisted that I apply to complete my master's degree. I was so excited. I could hardly wait to share the news with my husband. By this time, he had built us a new home and I had my desk in the future breakfast nook. It was always covered with books and papers, which would horrify my current husband who is, as our granddaughters describe, "a neat freak." No one ever commented on the mess or asked how my studies were progressing. That should have been hint number one. My schooling was like an elephant in the middle of the living room. Herb did not share his feelings for a few months. He bought our youngest daughter a horse. He bought our son a dirt bike, and he took our eldest daughter to Holland for a vacation before he told me that he would not support my continuing studies. He waited so long to tell me that I had received notification from the university about a scholarship they were offering me to attend the master's program. A professor from the university had applied for it on my behalf. I was unaware that I was even being considered for a scholarship, but it allowed me to calmly tell my husband that I did not need his support.

That was the beginning of the end. Herb and I went for counselling. The long daily drives in the winter months became unbearable. The first time I tried to leave, I wanted to take all three of our children. The older ones were finishing high school and wanted to stay near their friends. After learning about all the things that I did wrong in raising our children in my early psychology classes, I knew how critical high school and friends were at their age, so I agreed that they could stay with their dad. He was not a bad man. We just grew and developed different visions. Our youngest daughter came with me and to this day recalls those years as some of the best times of her life.

Lori would accompany me on my trips to the library and the university. Computers were just being introduced so I would sit her down in front of a computer and teach her just what she needed to know to enter and record my data. She was never shy, and if she did not understand how to do something, she would ask the university students in the computer lab how you did this or how you did that. They, of course, laughed at this little person with big glasses whose feet couldn't even reach the floor asking them how to do complicated computer tasks.

Lori and I had a two-bedroom apartment in a building that was filled mostly with students. I could cook. They could not. Our apartment was always an open house at mealtime with everyone bringing something to enhance the meal—bread, dessert, salad. It reminded me of being at home with Mom welcoming anybody and everybody who needed a meal, a cup of tea, or just some conversation. Lori loved hobnobbing with graduate students and had lots of help with any challenges that she encountered with her grade 6 homework.

Chapter Five

I'VE ONLY JUST BEGUN
(YEARS 40 TO 49) 1985-1994

In my late thirties I read a book called *A Population of One* by Canadian author Constance Beresford-Howe. The main character is overshadowed by her husband. They have a nice house and a nice family. She should have been happy, but to quote the popular singer Reba McIntyre, she wondered 'if there's life out there.' At 65 years of age, she received her first pension check from the government. She walked out and created a life of her own. It was not a great life, but it was her life. If my memory serves me right, at one point in time she was living on the street. But she built herself a circle of friends, and she was happy.

I remember the book well because it taught me that you can begin your life at any age. The world opened before me, and forty was no longer 'too old' to begin. I love to share, and when one of my employees was going through a rough time in her marriage, I bought this book for her. I wanted her to see that she had a lot of time to grow and develop into the person she wanted to be. She came to me after reading the book and asked if I was suggesting that she leave her husband.

I never gave the book as a gift again. People see different things. She and her husband did eventually separate and divorce and she did begin again. I have no idea whether the book influenced that decision or not.

My field of study at university was Community Psychology. We learned how to move into an organization, design and deliver a needs assessment, develop a program, evaluate it, and move on. I understood the concept immediately and I loved it. However, it took me twenty-five years to learn that society did not always appreciate the 'change' and 'move on' part. Everyone wanted to maintain the status quo, especially when money, jobs, and power were at stake. This was how things were done, and this is how things will be done forever. We will just improve the wheel!

There were only a few students in the program that I was in, and I often wonder what became of their lives and their careers. We took some classes with Experimental Psychology students because their numbers were small as well. I was living an interesting life. Brett and Lisa were in their teens and came to visit regularly. Lori was a preteen and precocious.

Sandra was living in a 2-bedroom apartment with our mom and dad who made sure that she had a roof over her head and food on the table. Mom always loved to feed everyone. Sandra worked at Colgate-Palmolive on the assembly line and complained about how much they wasted, throwing out dented tubes of toothpaste and soap. One Sunday in September, Sandra called and asked if I meant what I said in her birthday card. I could hear our mom giggling in the background. I had sent Sandra a lottery ticket and told her that any winning under $100 was hers to keep. Anything over, we shared. She said, "What about $100 even?" I said, "It's all yours," and she and mom squealed with delight.

One of my favorite stories about the master's level program involved a nun who had gone for three interviews to gain admission into the program. Her application was declined at each interview. The fourth time she arrived dressed in full habit and was admitted. 'Who knew that a nun's habit was the ultimate power suit?'[2] Clever woman!

Sitting in the psych lounge one day, we saw a posting for a contract position to evaluate the Standards and Guidelines for Children's Residential Facilities across the province of Ontario. We looked at the posting and four of us looked at each other and said, "We could do that." We developed a proposal and submitted it. Four weeks later our new company, Human Service Research Consultants, had their first, and I should add, *only*, government contract. Our firm analyzed documents, policies, and questionnaire results.

Pete, one of my fellow students, and I authored the final report of the Children's Residential Standards Review Project which presented results and

---

[2] *And Then There Were Nuns*, Jane Christmas, page 65

made recommendations to the Ministry of Community and Social Services (MCSS). We were successful, but we were so close to graduating and accepting positions in various locations across the province that it was not feasible to continue. Our company consisted of two young female graduate students, me, and Pete. Pete was always over at our apartment doing revisions and writing. When he came in one day and said that he had to move, I suggested that he move in with Lori and me. Lori moved into my bedroom, leaving Pete with a bedroom and private bathroom of his own. It sounded like the perfect solution. I had exhausted my scholarship money and teaching assistantships were rare. There was a little money from our contract with the Ministry but even that had to be split four ways. Pete paid rent. Lori and I had money for extras. However, the day after we had come to an agreement, I went to class only to be asked if it were true that Pete lived with me. Pete was young enough to be my son, but he sat there smiling and basking in the gossip. I always corrected the comments by saying, "Pete is renting a room from me," but not before noticing the raised eyebrows.

I called my mom every Sunday but always made sure that I had time for a few words with Sandra. Christine lived close by with Candy and supported mom with any day-to-day difficulties she encountered with Sandra. I probably didn't pay as much attention to Christine's complaints about Sandra as I should have because they always came across as blame.

When Sandra was in her early thirties living in Toronto, a gang of boys savagely beat her. Knowing Sandra, she fought back. They took her shoes and her jacket. Her jaw was broken, and she was left for dead.

One afternoon I received a desperate phone call from Christine. She and our mom were in the emergency department of a Toronto hospital. She wanted me to talk to the doctor and have Sandra committed to the psychiatric ward. I asked the doctor if Sandra could speak and if she would hand the phone to her. The doctor complied, and even though Sandra was hard to understand, I asked her how she liked *Wuthering Heights*, a book we were sharing and discussing at the time. We spent the next two to three minutes discussing the characters of Heathcliff and Catherine before she handed the phone back to the doctor.

At the end of that conversation, I was able to say that yes, Sandra has been diagnosed as suffering from schizophrenic tendencies, but she was not psychotic now. The doctor agreed with me. Sandra was admitted to a general ward. In defense of our mom and Christine, I did not see Sandra's face swollen to twice its size and black and blue from the vicious kicking. Despite everything, Sandra and I were able to connect

Lori and Pete were like siblings. He taught her to play chess and when she lost, she would sweep all the chess pieces onto the floor. There was more than one occasion when I had to ground her from playing chess for a week. Once at mealtime, they were trying to gross one another out with their mouths full of milk. I looked at each of them and started to laugh, causing my mouthful of milk to come out my nose. In unison they yelled, "She wins!"

When I was going to be late driving home from our office at the Ministry of Community and Social Services in Toronto, I would call one of the other master level students living in the building and ask if they could collect Lori after school and keep her with them until I got home. No problem. I could cook and they loved to eat.

Around this same time, Lori's dad informed us that he was going to have to put Duchess, Lori's beagle, down. Duchess was a full size black and tan beagle with long floppy ears and beautiful brown eyes. Duchess hated that we left her and became extremely disruptive. She destroyed anything that was left on the floor and used Herb's side of the bed as her personal toilet. Duchess blamed Herb for our absence. Lori was devastated. Not only did she have to leave her horse and her cat, but now her dog was going to be put down.

I shared my dilemma with Pete who suggested that we rent a townhouse. He knew another undergraduate student who was looking for a room to rent and by dividing the rent three ways we would be able to manage the townhouse and bring the beagle to Waterloo to live with us. So, Lori and I ended up living with two men! We worked. We played. We window shopped and sang "Islands in the Stream" as we walked to and from the mall. We held parties to celebrate significant dates throughout the year with Lisa and Brett joining us whenever they could.

I was tired of hearing my siblings blame Sandra for her challenges and frustrated that I couldn't find a reason other than alcohol or drugs. Sandra and I talked regularly about politics, history, and books that we shared.

The focus of my master's thesis was the development of an attendance program for truants. I needed a break from studying death and dying. While

I was working with the Waterloo Board of Education (who had hired ex-policemen as truant officers), the absentee rate continued to climb.

My interest in the program stemmed from a year-long field placement working with an attendance counselor at the Waterloo Board of Education. As a participant-observer, I was able to examine how the attendance department functioned. As the year progressed, it became increasingly evident that school attendance counsellors were functioning in a burnout environment and children were being underserviced. The needs of children had changed over the years. It was rare for a parent to keep a child home for the purpose of putting that child to work, and problems with little boys running off to fish were virtually nonexistent. Children's difficulties were far more complex and abstract than any faced by early professionals. The role of the attendance counselor became vague and all-encompassing. Their role was to counsel children on attendance, but attendance was not the problem. Nonattendance was a manifestation of one or more complex problems.

In my first year with the program, I was the only university student to meet with children who had been identified as being at risk for nonattendance. Following that, I designed, co-ordinated, and supervised an intervention program utilizing several university students who met with children who had been identified as being at risk for nonattendance. In the third year the Waterloo County Board's attendance counselors supervised the university volunteers. I acted in a consulting capacity. My understanding is that the program evolved over the years and professional social workers eventually replaced university volunteers.

Life continued in the townhouse. Lisa and Brett came down from Mount Forest whenever they could. Lori and I walked Duchess around the complex two to three times a day and when we sat looking out of the patio doors at the back of the house, we watched a beautiful Doberman Pincher wandering in his backyard right behind us. I felt content and safe. Who was going to bother us with two grown men living in the house? But then I had not yet met Barry.

Barry was the owner of the beautiful black and tan Doberman named Ebony. He was divorced and his eldest son BJ, who was ten years old, lived with him. Barry worked all day managing a local electrical firm and sold heating units at night to supplement his income.

One day there was a knock at the door and there stood Barry asking if I had a 15-year-old daughter who babysat.

I said, "No. You're at the wrong house. She lives next door."

"Doesn't your daughter babysit?"

"Yes. But she's only twelve," I answered.

"That's good enough," he said, and Barry hired my twelve-year-old daughter to babysit his ten-year-old son for the evenings he went out to sell.

Barry pumped Lori for information whenever she babysat. She would call after he left and say, "Mom, Barry asked if you go out on dates."

I laughed until one day Lori came home and said, "Guess where we're going Friday after school?"

"Where?" I could hear the excitement in her voice.

"Barry's taking BJ and you and I horseback riding and out for dinner!

Lori had to leave her horse in Mount Forest, so she was excited to go riding.

"He is, is he?" What else could I say?

Barry ended up cooking dinner for us on September 12th, 1984. To this day, he apologizes for burning the mushrooms. I was so impressed that he cooked dinner for us that I don't think I even noticed.

Two weeks later he asked me to go out with him to Toronto for dinner. We went to Ed's Warehouse on King Street and had a wonderful evening. Having just come out of one relationship and knowing that there were still things I wanted to do, I thanked him at the end of the evening and said, "My kids come first, then school, and if there is any time left, we can go out." He agreed, and we started to date.

Two months later, Pete and I were invited to do a presentation on the Young Offenders Act at the National Associations Active in Criminal Justice Seminar in Ottawa. In addition to working as a manager for an electrical company, Barry took on the added responsibility of caring for Lori and BJ as well as Ebony the Doberman and Duchess the beagle while we were gone. Shortly thereafter, Lori, Duchess and I moved across the backyard to live with Barry, BJ, and Ebony.

On September 12th, 1987, three years after Barry burned the mushrooms, we were married in the most beautiful house that I had ever seen. Barry built it, of course. Our five children were our attendants, along with Barry's 5-year-old niece Jennifer. Lori and Kathleen, Barry's youngest sister, sang "Until the 12th of Never." They had practiced separately for months and when they practiced together the night before the wedding, they sounded horrible!

Barry said, "What are we going to do?"

I said, "Let them sing."

To our surprise, when they sang during the service, their voices blended like angels. The fire alarm went off during the ceremony and Brett, our eldest son who was apprenticing as an electrician, shared his credentials with all the wedding guests, then left the ceremony to turn off the alarm. The police came because a neighbor living on the hill behind the house lodged a noise complaint.

By the time they arrived, the neighbor had joined the party and was dancing with my mom. The police were invited in as well but said they would return after shift.

The wedding guests lined up in the back park waiting for a helicopter to arrive and whisk us away. The helicopter was an embroidered truth that Barry shared to distract our guests so that we could escape via limousine out the front door. But anyone who knows Barry would not have been surprised to see a helicopter land.

The icing on the cake was when Barry received a beautifully wrapped wedding gift containing a single bullet with a note from my brother, Bob. The note said, "If you don't treat my sister well, the next one will come faster."

I like to use a quote from Albert Einstein when referring to Barry. "Life is like riding a bicycle. To keep your balance, you must keep moving." Barry and I have shared more than 38 years together. With our children, (Lisa, Brett, Lori, BJ and Jason,), Barry Thur and Charlotte Gibson became Thur/Gibson & Company. There have been good times, tough times, happy times, and sad times. Throughout it all, Barry keeps moving and making his to do lists with little boxes that never seem to get all checked off. I do believe that he thinks he will outwit the 'grim reaper' by keeping an ongoing list that never gets completed. Life with Barry is a whirlwind of activity, sights, scenes, and surprises. It's like living with an adrenaline junkie.

I have coined three descriptors of Barry over the years. I have described him as "coloring outside the lines," "embroidering the truth," and most recently as "failing retirement."

Pete was still very much on the scene. At our wedding, his gift of wine accompanied the following poem.

Dearest Charlotte and Barry

Since you first met, a few years it's bin,
(I knew you'd grow weary of living in sin)
In this great new house, and with pretty neat jobs,
You've left behind townhouses (& us Laurier slobs!)
Loved and respected, and admired by all,
Just stick by each other and you'll never fall.
So now that you're hitched up, and settled for good,
Just maintain the old fire, keep throwing on wood
Practice makes perfect & perfect is nice,
The secret of marriage is (so I'm told) the romantic spice
So, enjoy this here bubbly, when you're all alone,
And the kids are elsewhere, and you've unplugged
*the phone! ***

Yours Very Truly, with Love
Pete C.

**If you could have lived in sin for a few more years, I would have gotten a job and could have bought a case of the damned stuff for you! Ah well, such as it is, sip slowly!!*

Sandra never made it to our wedding. She was in a rehabilitation program for drug and alcohol abuse. It was in this program that she became infatuated with Flo, one of her counselors. Sandra was always searching for a way to improve her life and become 'balanced' or 'normal'. Our mom loved Sandra along with the rest of us, but Sandra was her baby. When Sandra said marijuana helped her cope with her difficulties, Mom grew a marijuana plant on her balcony and said it was because she loved the look of the leaves.

Before I graduated, I was finishing our contract with the Ministry of Health, completing my practicum placement with the Attendance Department at the Waterloo Board of Education, and authoring my thesis. The Heart and Stroke Foundation offered me a position in Waterloo as an area co-ordinator working with volunteers. The position was to start May 1st. I had two full months of work to complete and did not know how I was going to manage.

Barry said, "Take the job. I will look after everything at home: cooking, cleaning, and kids, but when everything else is complete, I want you to do something for me."

I said, "Yes," not even asking what he wanted and took the job.

Two months later, Barry and I signed up for a scuba diving course! I was not in my comfort zone, but "a promise is a promise," I kept repeating as I donned the heavy equipment. As it turns out, I am extremely buoyant and an excellent swimmer. Barry swims like a rock.

In our pool test, we had to go and sit on the bottom of the deep end of the pool with all our equipment on, take all our equipment off, swim to the surface, dive down, and put all our equipment back on. Barry, of course, could sit on the bottom with no equipment. I kept bouncing to the surface. Once on top, there was no way I could get back down to put on my equipment. One of our instructors had to dive down and pick up my weight belt to allow me to dive down and put the rest of my equipment on.

Our open water testing saw the team jog to shore fully equipped while I crawled on my hands and knees wearing four times the weight of the others. But I did it. I became certified and what I learned stays with me to this day. Scuba diving is relaxing. Yoga enthusiasts spend thousands of dollars trying to focus on their breathing and only on their breathing. When you are underwater and dependent on external apparatus to breathe, you focus on nothing else but air coming in and air going out.

We would rush home from work, have supper, and rush to our lesson. I'd enter the pool exhausted from a full day at work, but after an hour of focused breathing, I exited refreshed and ready to tackle any challenges that the next day presented.

I was hired as an Area Co-ordinator for the Heart and Stroke Foundation of Ontario in May 1985. I was responsible for the Regional Municipality of Waterloo, a position I held for the next two years. Contrary to what most people think, the Heart and Stroke Foundation was and is more than a fundraising organization. Fundraising was a part of it and our region raised more than $750,000. My responsibilities included managing all activities through a volunteer network (including recruitment), motivation of volunteers and staff, supervision of staff, public relations, public education, and office administration.

During round one of the position interviews, one of the executive volunteers asked if I played golf.

"No," I replied.

"Then how do you propose to recruit volunteers?" was her next question.

I shared all my experience with the recruitment of volunteers which must have made an impression because I was invited to the next round of the interview process.

The Director of Regional Services drove in from Toronto. The Regional Manager drove in from Niagara and I met with the two senior staff women who were to decide my future. When I told Barry that I got the position, he was proud and asked the next most relevant question, "How much will you earn?" I told him $17,000 a year. He laughed and said that he earned double that amount with no university degree. I calmly responded that I had only just begun.

Many months later, my Regional Manager shared that the Director of Regional Services advised her against hiring me. She said that I was too ambitious and wouldn't stay long in the position. She was right. Two years later I took over my Regional Manager's position and was responsible for managing the whole of West Central Region.

I went into the office every morning to spend time with each of the existing volunteers and to learn what they did and what they thought we could do to improve the operation. They were shocked to be asked. I was equally shocked to learn that many of them volunteered for two to four days a week.

One sweet lady came in like clockwork and worked from nine until five every day except for Wednesday. After a few weeks I asked what she did on Wednesday, and she told me that she had her hair done. I said that I was not complaining but simply curious about why she put in so many volunteer hours. Her answer is still with me today.

She said, "If you don't use it, you lose it," as she pointed to her head.

Some volunteers missed days to have their hair done, others missed days to play golf. And some 'volunteered' to fulfill a requirement.

Early in my career working with volunteers, I agreed to host placements from the John Howard Society. The John Howard Society supported individuals who ran into trouble with the law and were given a number of hours of community service rather than a jail sentence. The gentleman that I was asked to place had been charged with stealing. I was working for a fundraising organization, and we took in a lot of cash. I asked what he had stolen. He had been charged with stealing a loaf of bread because he was hungry and had no money. I never hesitated and asked to speak with him on the phone. He had a marvelous, calm voice. He had been a bank manager and had recently been diagnosed as bipolar. He lost his job with the bank. We were heading into a heavy residential fundraising campaign period. I thought that he would be great on reception. He had a magnificent voice, and he could free-up my experienced receptionist to do cold calls for door-to-door canvassing recruitment. I had a whole office full of volunteers, mostly female and mostly elderly, but everyone was not comfortable soliciting over the phone. They had their specific jobs and that is all they wanted to do.

Our new volunteer staff person arrived Monday morning, and he was the scariest looking individual I had ever seen. His hair was long and needed washing. His clothes were unkempt and needed washing. He also needed a shave and some deodorant. I left my pristine receptionist where she was and moved our newest 'volunteer' to the back-storage room with a phone and lists of names and numbers to call and try and recruit. He was bright and needed little instruction. He quickly grasped what was required of him. He knew how many hours he had to work and kept close track of his obligation. Within a few days he was not only having an extremely high success rate recruiting canvassers, but I soon heard laughter and chatter from the back room as our office volunteers became comfortable with our newest addition. Day by day he started to clean up his appearance and by the time his placement was complete, he was looking good, interacting with others, and proud of his success rate.

Before you start thinking that I was a miracle worker and that is all it takes to turn a street person suffering from problems with living into a stable member of society, let me share our final celebration. I took our transformed, almost jail bird to a fancy restaurant for a final farewell celebration to thank him for recruiting the largest number of canvassers our region had ever seen. He looked at me with the most civilized look he could muster, and with his magnificent voice, he said, "You're welcome. But I still think you're an idiot to work for a living."

I still smile when I think of him and mentally thank him for kick-starting my success. That year Waterloo Region raised the most per capita residential funds in the province.

Barry and I started to meld our careers as well as our lives. I came home one night and was upset that my Annual Meeting Chairman resigned a month before the event. We sat, me with my glass of wine and Barry with his rum and Pepsi. After listening to my concerns, Barry said, "I can do it."

I asked if he had ever done anything like this in the past. He admitted that he had not, but he said that he knew how to organize and felt he could do it.

I said, "OK." I told him that I needed a great speaker on heart disease. Barry said that he used to drink at the Keon Hotel in Chapeau, Quebec. He would find out how to contact Dr. Keon, a well-known heart surgeon at the Heart Institute in Ottawa. His family owned the hotel, so Barry had something to talk to him about. He called up Dr. Keon's office and asked if he would be our guest speaker. He arranged for the Waterloo Inn to donate the facilities and a room for Dr. Keon, for the Party Place to donate red balloons that arched the pool, for Air Canada to donate the flight, and for a limousine service to pick up and return Dr. Keon to the airport the following morning so he would not miss his daughter's wedding!

Rick Gallop, the Executive Director of the Heart and Stroke Foundation, attended Waterloo Region's Annual meeting that year, so it was no surprise that I was offered the position of Regional Manager when our current Regional Manager took a position with another charity. For the next 20 years that I spent in the non-profit sector, I shared with audiences that one of my retention strategies was to marry my number one volunteer.

Sandra loved to hear stories about my work and my life.

When I applied for the Regional Manager position, I stipulated that the regional office must move from St. Catharines to Waterloo. I was, of course, told that there was no money.

No money. No problem. Through donations of materials, office supplies, desks, and floral accents, Barry turned our back-storage center into a beautiful Regional Manager's office.

Likewise, when Barry wanted to go moose hunting, he asked me to manage his construction company. I panicked and said that I knew nothing about construction. He said that it was just common sense, and he was right. He was not gone a day before the bricklayers called to say that it was raining and they couldn't lay brick outside. The supervisor was going to send everyone home. I said, "Just a minute. Is there any brickwork that needs to be done inside?"

"Yes, the fireplace," he said. I said, "Then start inside and move to the outside tomorrow when the rain stops."

We became a team. When HSFO visitors and dignitaries came to Waterloo, they always ended up at our home for one reason or another. They saw the quality and detail of Barry's work. Several commented that if we ever moved to Toronto, Barry was to call them. We did eventually move to Toronto and Barry did call them, launching a successful twenty-year career as a general contractor in the big city.

During this time, Sandra continued to move in and out of my life as she struggled to make a life of her own. She wrote, sent postcards, and visited when she was able.

I became a volunteer member of the Waterloo District Health Council and because of Sandra's issues, I chose to work first on the Mental Health Committee then on the Strategic Planning Committee, and finally, I chaired a committee called Women's Health Issues and Concerns.

I learned that I needed down time as well as stimulation, and as life settled into a two-income family, we started to plan vacations away. Knowing that I had something to look forward to kept me motivated and moving forward, both with my search to help Sandra and with the development of my credibility.

Our first trip was a one-week vacation to Jamaica. My mom, who was still well, came to stay with the kids and the critters. By this time Yoda, a seal point Siamese, had joined the family. Yoda ruled the house and kept both the beagle and the Doberman in their places. Sandra loved all the kids and animals that were in our lives.

In Jamaica, I thought Barry had gone deaf. We were in the hotel lobby, and he was exchanging money when a local resident approached him. All I could hear was Barry saying, "What, what, what?"

When he joined me, I asked if he couldn't hear what he was being asked. He said that he heard just fine but he couldn't believe that he was being propositioned to buy drugs. I guess it's not as big a deal today as it was then, but we were both shocked. Barry soon learned that to keep the drug peddlers away, he just had to tell them that he had bought too much and ask if he could sell some back to them.

I realized that I had to take better care of myself or I would be of no use to anyone. I still walked wherever I could, but I also added yoga classes to my routine to secure that ever elusive 'balance' everyone was always searching for and that I thought Sandra needed.

Mom dying was a turning point in our lives. I was still working as Regional Manager for West Central Ontario, but I was offered the additional responsibility of Assistant Director of Regional Services. I was to function as a Regional Manager with the added responsibility of being a trouble shooter for the Province of Ontario assessing and developing provincial programs in the areas of recruitment, orientation, training, recognition, and fundraising. These additional duties allowed me to travel to Toronto on a regular basis. That is where I wanted to be so that I could provide some support to Sandra and our mom when our mom became ill.

Our mom was funny. She always told me that she wanted a doctor in the family and after working with a local physician in Mount Forest for eight years, I knew the language and could ask the appropriate questions. She always asked me to accompany her when she had a doctor's appointment.

Our dad had died in 1983 and our mom died in 1990. At 45 years of age, I was an orphan. It may sound silly, but even after studying about death and dying, I was not prepared for the intense grief that I felt or how it surprised me.

My reading on the subject taught me that grieving is a process, and you must experience each special day or holiday throughout the year without your special person. Knowing that still did not prepare me. Our mom died on November 22, 1990. On Mother's Day 1991 while I was grocery shopping, I looked around the store and realized that I had no one to buy flowers for. I had to leave to hide my sobbing. I passed Barry's son BJ in the garage. He asked his dad what was wrong. When Barry explained, BJ went out and bought me flowers. He still wishes me Happy Mother's Day every year, but he bought me flowers when I needed them most.

My mom was one of the strongest women I have ever known. The biggest life lesson she ever taught me was to pay attention to details and don't judge. We were walking by a church fence one cold and snowy evening when I was about eight years old. There was what I perceived to be a drunken old man sitting on the ground clinging to the wrought iron fence posts. Everyone was walking by or looking the other way. I looked the other way. My mom looked directly at the elderly gentleman and said, "This man is sick." She called the police who immediately called an ambulance. They recognized that he was going into a diabetic coma. I asked how she knew. She said that she looked at him and she saw the fear in his eyes.

Mom became a shop steward with a powerful union. She was always looking out for the welfare of employees. She continued to influence my behavior throughout my employment years.

My new position with the province required staff changes, and as much as I admired and trusted my mom's opinion, I would never call upon her when I had to terminate an employee.

I became a manager, a Vice-President, and eventually the CEO of a major organization. It was my job to make sure that the city, the region, and the province succeeded. I knew and respected my mom's feelings and direction so much so that she never really knew what I did but because of her, I tried to ensure that my terminations were all delivered with compassion.

When Mom was dying, and I was working from her apartment, I heard her talking to a friend about me. She said, "I am not exactly sure what Charlotte does, but I do know she does paperwork all day, and then she gets all dressed up at night, goes out and comes back with a lot of money."

In addition to managing staff in the fundraising organization, I wrote proposals and developed strategic directions. In the evenings, I attended golf tournaments, galas, and conventions where various groups donated substantial amounts of money to ensure the success of the organization. I often wondered what my mother's friends thought I did with my evenings.

Mom was the reason I accepted the position of Vice-President of Regional Services in July of 1990, a position I held until December 1997. As the senior administrative staff person for field services, my responsibilities included raising $25.5 million from the field. There were and still are many other avenues of revenue generation. When I moved into the position of Vice-President of Regional Services, there were thirty-five chapters of volunteers doing the field work across the province. When I moved on to another organization, the number of chapters had grown to exceed one hundred.

This was the second of three major career moves that I was to make in this decade. Mom was the first of three family deaths to occur during that time. Our dad had died in 1983 and I was sad, but it was nothing like the loss I felt when our mom died. Mom's passing left a huge void in the family and a huge responsibility. Her final words to my sister Christine and I were, "Take care of each other." We knew that she wanted us to stay close, but we also knew that she wanted us to take care of our youngest sister Sandra.

Chapter Six

GOOD ENOUGH IS THE ENEMY OF EXCELLENCE (YEARS 50 TO 55)1995-1999

Both Barry and I planned hard, we worked hard, and we played hard. Mom never saw the large home that Barry built in Toronto, but she was in our beautiful home in Waterloo, so she knew how talented he was. My sister-in-law Helen described Barry as having 'magic hands.' She didn't see the Toronto house completed either. She died at 61 from a blood clot after hiatus hernia surgery. I moved back to Toronto to be close to my family just as my family began to shrink.

After reading Sandra's letters and journal, it was obvious that she struggled with demons from an early age. Our mom died of colon cancer at age 70 in 1990. Up until that point, our mom provided for Sandra, who lived with her in an apartment in the east end of Toronto.

After our mom died, Sandra continued to live in the two-bedroom apartment by herself. It was too big and held too many memories, both happy and sad. She moved to a bachelor suite in the same complex. Her friends started taking advantage of her, staying all night, and helping themselves to her belongings. Sandra moved into an apartment above a donut store across the street from the building and then finally into a room at Christine's house.

Sandra started to write in her late thirties and early forties. She made lists and wrote letters, limericks, and poems to try and express her thoughts and feelings. Her sketches are more difficult to interpret but she continually tried to communicate what she was feeling as she tried to focus on her journey to find balance.

I often spoke around the province, recruiting and motivating volunteers. My preferred topic was stress. My favorite quote was the title of a book by Hans Selye, *Stress, Is It Worth Dying For?* I would ask half of the audience to stand and half to sit. I asked them to look at the other half, and then I would say, "Half of you will die from either heart disease or stroke."

It was a powerful message, and I received many compliments on how I delivered it and how I never looked at my notes. Little did they know that I couldn't see my notes without my glasses, so I always had to memorize everything I wanted to say, leaving me free to look directly at the audience.

I was aware that I experienced stress too, and after several years of taking yoga, I eventually learned that I needed to invest in myself daily. No matter how busy I was or how difficult it was, I needed to find ways to continually make sure that I didn't burn out. I would be of no use to anyone, not even myself, if I couldn't stand alone and lend a helping hand. The more personally fulfilled I am, the more I'm heading where I want to be, the more I can give to others (*Inc. Your Dreams*, Rebecca Maddox, 1995, p. 21).

This was the hardest concept I had ever tried to share. We want to sacrifice. We want to be martyrs. We want everyone to love us and say what a good person we are. Few consider that they must take care of themselves to be strong enough to help others.

Our house in Toronto was built after three years of commuting from Waterloo to Toronto and back again the same day. I wanted to live in Toronto to be near my family and kept telling Barry about the Population Geography course that I had taken years before. I learned that many people who lived in the city moved to the suburbs because the housing was less expensive. However, all the conveniences—subways, streetcars, hospitals, specialists—were in the city. When their children left home, the families who had moved to the outskirts could no longer afford to move back into the city center because it had become too expensive.

At exactly this point in our lives, the recession hit. The price of houses dropped in both cities. Fewer people needed homes built in Waterloo. As my career sped up Barry, moved from Mr. Contractor and took care of our home as Mr. Mom, which I might add he was extremely good at. He was a little too strict for me, evidenced by the fact that all our children moved out of the family home as soon as they were able.

Barry asked BJ, his eldest son, to clean up his room once and then twice. The next day when BJ came home from school, everything that had been on the floor of his room went out the window and greeted him on the front lawn. I know the years haven't changed Barry much, because when we recently (2016) told our granddaughters that we were bringing home a surprise for them from Florida and the hint was that "Grandpa hates them," Erica replied, "Then it has to be dirt or a mess because Grandpa hates both of them." They each got a sweatshirt with Minions on it and began to talk like the characters so that Barry couldn't understand a word they said.

The nineties saw our children leave the nest. Lisa went to York University to study Women's Issues. I should have realized that university can be daunting for a young person who had grown up in a small village. I grew up in Toronto and went to university as an adult student. I was excited. I loved it. I thought that we were giving Lisa a wonderful opportunity at an age when she could build a circle of friends that would last a lifetime.

Brett came to live with us right after he completed high school, and even though he had a choice of which university he wanted to attend, he said, "Mom, I don't know what I want to do. If I go to university now, I would be wasting my time and your money."

Barry managed an electrical firm at the time and offered him a job as an electrical helper. Brett lived with us for a brief time. He couldn't stand the rules either.

One day he came to me and said, "Mom, Barry signed me up as an apprentice. I don't know what I want to do, but I don't want to be an electrician."

I said, "Just humor him until you decide what you want to do."

Three years later, Brett received his license as an electrician. Two years after that he was a firefighter for the City of Waterloo. There were one thousand applicants for only two positions within the Fire Department. Brett came to me and asked for help with his interview.

I said, "I will help you, but you must promise to do everything I say."

He agreed, and I ran him through several mock interviews. I asked him to go to the library and read everything he could about the Waterloo Fire Department.

He said, "Aw, Mom." I reminded him of his promise. I also told him that he was going into this process with three strikes against him. He was male, white, and young. He secured one of the two positions. When asked by the hiring panel if he had anything else to add at the end of the interview, he commented that when he went to the library, he was impressed to learn that the Waterloo Fire Department had not had a single death on the job. The interview panel all laughed. Two years later, he was working laying computer wire for Manulife Financial on his days off from the fire department. Several years later, he became Vice-President of the Waterloo Region Firefighters Union and then President, which would have made my mom beam with pride.

Lori went to Wilfrid Laurier University. She dropped out and moved to Toronto to live close to where Barry and I were living. She worked for a year and then moved to the Niagara Region to go to Brock University where she graduated with a degree in English.

Lori was the first of our children to marry and give us a grandchild a few years later. Enter Ethan, stage right! What a window to a wonderful new world. It would change the whole direction of my life in a few years, allowing me more time to follow up with Sandra's activities.

In Waterloo, both BJ and Lori worked at a grocery store part-time while they were going to high school. Even though Lori had been his babysitter, they remain lifelong friends. BJ had a stormy exit from the family home which was now in Toronto.

Jason, Barry's youngest son, was only four when Barry and I met. Jason lived with his mother and stepfather in Petawawa. He was a cutie and I loved seeing the world through the eyes of a four-year-old again. For many years, Jason only visited during the holidays. Academics were not his strongest point. He loved the outdoors, fishing, and, later, hunting.

Once he reached his teen years, I noticed him smoking on more than one occasion when he came for a visit. He knew I worked for the Heart and Stroke Foundation and that I was dead set against smoking. One summer he came down to Toronto and made a point of saying that he no longer smoked. He made several other comments, more like hints, which started me thinking. I told Barry that I thought Jason wanted to move in with us. BJ was gone and, whereas it was just a bungalow, we did have a vacant spare room in the basement. Even though he was not four anymore, we still had a bond that had developed over the years. Jason moved in and finished his last year of the high school within walking distance of our home. He went to George Brown College first for business and then for graphic arts. He graduated with a diploma, but unfortunately, no job, just a ton of debt. Eventually with a push from his dad and assistance from his brother BJ, Jason ended up with an Elevator Mechanic's certification as well.

The children and Sandra wove themselves in and out of our lives as Barry and I moved forward with our careers. Sandra loved that we were living in Toronto. She used public transit to visit and come for meals. If no one was home, she would leave notes or lottery tickets in our mailbox. Barry never begrudged the time I spent with Sandra. He would save all his empty beer and alcohol bottles and it would become an outing for Sandra and me to visit the beer store and turn in the empties for some extra money to boost her pocket change.

I definitely wasn't Sandra's only support. She wrote about Christine buying her a winter coat, Bob and Shirley taking her for pancake breakfasts, and visiting Joe, and his wife Helen, for tea. Her niece and godchild, Candy and her husband Sam were particularly good to Sandra. She lived with them for a short while and Sandra commented with fondness about going enumerating with Candy. Years later when she was living at Bendale Acres, a long-term care facility, Sandra would tell me that Candy's children came to visit. Candy had two daughters. Children of all ages and color volunteered at Bendale. In Sandra's eyes and mind, they were all Candy's children.

Family members may have been frustrated with her at times, but we were a family and Sandra was always included at birthdays and celebrations. She wrote that after mom died, Nicole (Shirley and Bob's daughter) wanted to buy mom's TV and converter for $100. Sandra said that she would probably just give it to her because Nicole was family.

Our house in Toronto was built over seven years. Barry is the most meticulous person I know when it comes to building and detail. Accompanying Barry as we made material choices caused me to learn more about 'window mullions' than I ever wanted to know. We built the garage in the first year to house all of Barry's tools. We then started on landscaping and fencing in year two to keep our Doberman and beagle safe. Our backyard became an extension of our home. You would never believe that you were in the city of Toronto when you were sitting in the treed garden at the back of the house. The main house had to wait for both finances and time to become available. In the third and fourth year, we renovated the basement. The focus was Barry's office with a walkout to the backyard so that tradespeople could come and go without walking through the main part of the house. There was a second bathroom, bedroom, laundry room, and galley kitchen built in the basement. Our long-range plan was to hire someone to take care of us in our old age and provide them with separate living quarters. The plumbing, venting, and mechanics were installed and capped off at the main floor level to be connected when the final structure was built. Our new basement provided us with all the necessities required to allow us to manage while we built upstairs. We took year five off and explored what seemed like a million options for our build. In year six we connected our half-renovated house to city supplies (water, sewage, electricity). We were finally ready. Word spread fast about Barry's talent and speed. A TV show called "This Small Space" wanted to film the construction of the house, but Barry moved too quickly after so much planning, and they had to settle for an interview once we moved in. I left for a conference in Prince Edward Island in the last week of May. When I returned a week later, the old house was gone, and the new house was up to the second floor. It took 12 weeks to erect from concept to completion. We were surprised when our house was featured in Better Homes and Gardens in Japan. I couldn't read the words, but the pictures captured everything.

I continued to work my army of volunteers hard. I had 60,000 door-to-door canvassers across the province and that one program raised more than five million dollars. Bob Luba, one of the Heart and Stroke volunteer presidents, called me General Schwarzkopf and would salute me whenever we met. Previously the organization went to sleep over the summer months. I turned the summer months into a time of preparation, recruitment, and training so that every office was ready to move into high gear in the fall. The fall became a 'fill in the blanks' period with a rest over Christmas, in preparation for the move into high gear during February (Heart Month).

There were numerous volunteers and as many stories about them but just as my John Howard Society volunteer kicked off the success of my first position, there was one lady who made me smile throughout my latter years with HSFO.

Her name was Jane. Jane was a volunteer when I started as Vice-President of Regional Services. She was very British, and most staff and volunteers did not associate with her. I never knew why. She was a diligent worker, but she was a little different. She reminded me of a high functioning Sandra. She did like to talk, and my feeling was that our volunteers saved us hundreds of thousands of dollars. The least I could do was to spare a few words of encouragement and show some interest in them as human beings. Jane was a whiz on the computer and while she was not fully qualified to be an executive assistant, she carried the load during staff vacancies on many occasions. I'm not exactly sure how she managed financially because she volunteered daily. She may have been on a disability pension or some other financial aid. It was none of my business and I never pursued it. I continued to treat her like an employee.

I treated all our volunteers like staff. I refused to let them describe themselves as 'just a volunteer.' I always corrected them and said that in my department the only difference between a volunteer and a staff person was a paycheck. My expectation of them was the same. Many asked for references when they looked for employment and some even asked if I would give them a performance appraisal. I always did. Jane did not fall into the regular realm of volunteer. She had one habit that embarrassed me on more than one occasion, but now it only makes me smile. Jane would serve me tea on a silver platter every afternoon at 3:00 P.M. I kept telling her it was not necessary, but she insisted. One afternoon, I was meeting with the CEO of the Heart and Stroke Foundation of Ontario. Our weekly meeting was usually in the morning, but because of other meetings, this one was scheduled from 2 to 4 P.M. in his corner office. At 3:00 P.M. sharp, Jane knocked on the door and walked in with a cup of tea on a silver platter for me and nothing for him. We laughed when Jane left, and he asked his administrative assistant if she would mind getting him a cup of tea.

Barry, however, has what he considers a much better story about Jane. We always had and still do have Christmas celebrations throughout the month of December. The players change on a yearly basis, but the celebrations continue. This particular year, I included Jane in the staff party festivities. At times she worked harder than paid staff. Jane arrived, gave Barry her coat and was wearing a very sheer black, dressy blouse. The problem was she wore no bra or light liner under the see through blouse. Looking through today's celebrity magazines, Barry says that Jane was just before her time. It was difficult but we suffered through the evening. All of my staff were female, as in most non-profits at the time, and all of them knew Jane. They took their cues from me, and we simply ignored her apparel which allowed her to keep her dignity. She had a wonderful time and raved at the office that she had been included in a staff celebration. Jane left Canada and ended up marrying an American who was imprisoned for downloading instructions from the internet on how to build a bomb! After Jane left for the United States, the only correspondence I ever received from her was an article her new husband had written on how to cure breast cancer.

Sandra had a lot of friends. She was very social and because there were only two years between Sandra and Christine, they were closer to each other as children than they were to me. They hung out with the same crowd, had the same friends, and slept in the same bedroom.

Sandra struggled to find some sense of balance and somewhere to belong. She moved between Alcoholic Anonymous and Spectrum, a community outreach program that supported individuals suffering from mental illness.

Sandra was always asking me what she could do. She did laundry and some cleaning to supplement her government income. I told her to write, journal, and draw, which she did. I asked if there was anything that she had always wanted to do and she said that she wanted to learn how to speak French. I suggested that she sign up for a night course. I paid, of course. Sandra often described falling in love with her doctor, teacher, or support worker. This was one such case when she fell in love with her French teacher. On the final night of the French class, everyone was going down to King Street to a French restaurant. Patrons ordered in French and were served French cuisine. At that time, I was the only person that Sandra knew who was able to read a French menu, order in French and, of course, pick up the tab. Sandra invited me along.

We had a wonderful evening. Because of Sandra's attire (jeans, plaid lumberjack shirt and a ball cap, before any of them were popular) and her difficulty learning French, she had been ostracized by her classmates. No one spoke with us. The teacher smiled at us. Sandra was bright and an adaptive learner. Jaws dropped around the table after I had quietly coached her in the proper pronunciation as she ordered her meal.

Sandra loved to eat out in restaurants and coffee shops. She said it made her feel human. I often joined her and of course paid for the meal. She frequented some seedy areas. One Christmas, Barry, the current love of my life, bought me a warm Roots jacket with a matching furry hat. The first time I wore it, Sandra and I sat down in one of her favorite breakfast restaurants and several men and women sitting near us changed seats to move further away from us.

I looked at Sandra and shrugged, "What's up?"

She said, "You look like a cop."

I laughed and thought nothing more of it until several Metro Police officers walked into the restaurant and tipped their hats to me. I had some armor to roam in seedy areas! I still have the outfit, but Roots discontinued it shortly after. They may have received the same feedback. Now, I only wear it when I want to be warm.

The only time I was uncomfortable accompanying Sandra was when she asked me to go with her to a dance that Spectrum had organized. Sandra was having a fun time and several members had asked me to dance. My first dance partner said that he had overcome drugs. I said, "That's nice." The second had been attending Gamblers Anonymous. Again, my response was, "That's nice, you should be proud."

The strange feeling I had, and one that both Sandra and I laughed about later that evening, was that I didn't have anything to overcome, and she hadn't overcome anything yet.

Sandra had a difficult life, but we were always able to polish the gems and let them shine through the heartache.

After our mom died, Sandra volunteered at both the Heart and Stroke Foundation and later the Easter Seals Society. I prepared my staff for her arrival by sharing that she may look like a street person, but that she was a kind, sweet woman and that she was my sister. I always made sure Sandra had a task that allowed her to be successful. She went to AA meetings, self-medicated, and tried to build her own circle of friends.

Sandra started writing eight weeks after we buried our mom. One of her first notations was an Alcoholics Anonymous reflection.

Dear God,

I have made a mess of my life so far. I pray I can be of service to a bigger cause than I can imagine. I pray to do your will.

Acceptance is the answer to all my problems today.

Now that we were living in Toronto, yoga became a big focus for me. I attended weekly classes. I needed balance and a distraction from the challenges of work, those surrounding Sandra, and raising a blended family. Sandra was continually looking for a place where she could live by herself

Yoga isn't about learning to do contorted poses. The ancient practice is an avenue for self-exploration and self-mastery. I needed that proficiency and that strength. I needed balance. I remember watching Steven Segal in a movie and commenting that his sense of presence extended beyond the size of the screen. He was there! You knew he was there. I wanted that visual strength. I shared my thoughts with Barry about how I loved the aura of strength that surrounded the man. Steven had a ponytail. Barry grew a ponytail. When I learned that in real life Mr. Segal had been charged with beating his wife, he quickly fell out of my favor. But to this day, Barry continues to sport the ponytail.

I worked in the position of Vice-President of Regional Services for seven years. For me, it was a long time in one position. My career philosophy was to stay in one position for only 3 to 5 years. If I wasn't moving up, I would be moving out. I was looking for a change.

I went to a company called Images That Suit and said, "Dress me like an Executive Director or President of a Company." They did, and I moved into my acting mode. I offered to take additional responsibilities off the Executive Director's plate and started sending out resumes. I did share my strategy with him. I told him that since he was older than me, he would have to retire first. I had never been through an Executive Director interview, and I wanted the experience. I had also observed over the years that Boards of Directors tended to bring in a new CEO from another company. They wanted to hire someone with innovative ideas and a new direction that would take their organization to the next level of success. At one point I was interviewing for three Executive Director positions at the same time: Canadian Hearing, Canadian National Institute for the Blind (CNIB), and Easter Seals. Canadian Hearing and CNIB hired from within, and I continued with my interviews with Easter Seals.

I made a big faux pas later that year when I attended a non-profit conference in downtown Toronto. I was going up the escalator for lunch and making conversation with the woman behind me. She said that she was with CNIB. I said, "Oh, they chose the wrong candidate to be Executive Director."

She then said, "They chose me!"

I made sure that I sat with her over lunch and tried to make light of the fact that I had put my foot in my mouth. She laughed and said that I might be right. She was finding the position extremely difficult, but CNIB bylaws stated that if there are two candidates who are equally qualified, but one was legally blind, the committee must choose the one with the disability. She was legally blind. She was kind and did make me feel better, but I've never forgotten that life lesson. My mother's words, "If you have nothing good to say, say nothing," came back to haunt me.

Sandra was also looking for a change. She tried to do Grade 12 Economics by correspondence but felt that the course was too difficult for her. She sent the package back. In her writing she shared that she had a desire to become a labor lawyer.

I came. I went. I moved out of the city. I moved back into the city. I changed partners but I always loved my family. Bob and Joey were my strength. They divided the 'Dad' responsibilities. Dad was my first dad. My brothers were my second. We had a strong bond. So strong, in fact, that Bob asked me to sit with him while he received the Last Rights before he died.

Bob and Shirley, his wife, were arguing at the time and no one really believed that Bob was dying. I remember sitting with him in his living room the entire day. A red cardinal flew onto the front veranda and sat at the window for at least twenty minutes. I kept talking to Bob about how remarkable it was that the bird just sat there looking in. Shirley came home from work and said that he needed to go to the hospital. He looked at me, and I said, "I'm not leaving until I know that you are safe and cared for in the hospital." He died on the way to the hospital in the ambulance. Our brother Bob was the third death in the family, five years after our mom.

Sandra took each death hard.

This was the decade when I turned fifty. Barry had demonstrated his organizational ability many times over the years and my fiftieth birthday was no exception. He wanted to arrange a huge family dinner, totally catered in our backyard for both his family and mine and all our friends. Even though expressing my needs is sometimes difficult for me, I told Barry that he didn't really know who my close friends were. They lived all over the province. Some were friends from high school, others from university and still more from working or volunteering with me. There was even one from my previous life in Mount Forest. Barry asked for a list. He tracked down a handful of my closest friends that he was able to reach, then planned and executed a birthday weekend. Barry decorated our back yard with balloons and flowers. On the Saturday, my close friends and I were served a sit-down lunch in the yard. We wined and dined and shared stories spanning twenty years. I don't believe any of them knew each other before they arrived, but several became members of our weekend book club retreats for years to come. Saturday was amazing and Sunday was spectacular. All our children and their dates, brothers, sisters, nieces, nephews, neighbors, and friends arrived for an afternoon of celebration. Not to be outdone, my sister Christine made a phone call and twenty minutes later in walked a young, good-looking police officer in full uniform. If you think I was surprised at the sight of him, I was shocked when he proceeded to strip down to a skimpy black speedo and dance provocatively around the yard. It was a small yard. And this was how the curtain closed on my fifth decade.

Sandra was delighted. She even wore a dress with her wool work socks and high cut running shoes. We got a great picture of her that day looking balanced and happy, but we all knew that underneath the surface smiles, she continued with her struggles.

Leaving the Heart and Stroke Foundation was one of the most difficult moves I ever made. I had been employed in four different positions over thirteen years. I had built a wonderful staff structure, an industrious and dedicated volunteer army, and a magnificent field structure. I was proud of what I was leaving. I was always asking my senior management team to give me a brief of what they were proposing so that I could review it and give them feedback. On my last day with the organization, the provincial staff gathered in the boardroom and each member of my senior management team shared their best wishes for my future by hanging underwear that reflected their individual personality (briefs) on a clothesline that was hung across the front of the room.

CNIB was out, Canadian Hearing was out, but Easter Seals was still in the running. The interview process lasted 6 months, the longest one I had ever experienced. Every Friday a box would arrive at our home, and it would be filled with some background information and several questions. The following Tuesday night I met with the hiring committee and interviewers would ask how I would deal with different situations. As I presented my thoughts, I often wondered if they were working off months of severance that they had to pay my predecessor by having me manage the operations as part of the interview process. If true, it was a very clever strategy.

My first direction from the 'old board' was to replace the entire management team. In addition, I restructured the parent network to include representation from across the province as well as Easter Seal children who had become young adults. A board of directors of forty members was streamlined to nine. Seven Easter Seals' camps were reduced to two and a new program called 'Recreational Choices' was introduced. I'm sure that my mother turned over in her grave yet again as I wielded the broom across the organization to make room for a new direction.

A new Provincial Board of Directors developed the direction and strategy for the organization. A new Regional Board consisting of parents, Easter Seal young people, and committed community volunteers executed the plan at the local level across the province.

The organization still exists today so I did complete one objective, but I did not win any popularity contests with my views on merging Easter Seals and March of Dimes. I felt that those two organizations should be one providing support for the physically disabled from cradle to grave. March of Dimes has a totally different focus in the United States but in Canada they serve to support people over the age of eighteen living with disabilities participating fully in life on their own terms.

My thinking over the years expanded to include autism and several other debilitating disorders that affected both children and adults. I am sad when I walk our dog down the street and see a sign posted stating that autism is not just a childhood disorder. Children don't outgrow autism. I saw that twenty years ago but could not move the needle one inch in that direction. A grandmother with a grandson on the autistic spectrum recently asked me why it took so long for anyone to recognize and support this area of need. My answer was, "Because you can't see it." Everyone wanted to support disabilities that could be seen. Even Sandra's disability was not always visible or evident.

Because my strength and success have come from the volunteers who have supported me over the years, I will close my last salaried non-profit experience with a description of Alice, my volunteer and my friend.

Alice is one of my favorites. In her late seventies when I met her, she had never married. Her official title was Flight Officer Alice Hill of the Royal Canadian Air Force (RCAF) Women's Division from 1941 to 1945. Alice served in Ottawa and Toronto and was appointed MBE in 1944 for her work in setting up the system in No. 1 Service Flying Training school at Camp Borden, Ontario. In her later years Alice became a professional volunteer. She volunteered for The Heart and Stroke Foundation of Ontario, Ontario March of Dimes, Easter Seals Ontario, and Big Brothers and Big Sisters of Toronto. Alice was closest to her sister Sue and Sue's family. Sue had three sons. One was a volunteer Chairman of the Heart and Stroke Foundation Board of Directors, Dr. Tony Graham. Alice wanted to help the organization and thereby help her nephew, a very prominent clinical cardiologist. He came to me and asked if there was anything that his Aunt Alice could do. I said that I would investigate. I met with Alice, who was very crusty, and told me that she would not touch money. It was filthy. We were a fundraising organization, but of course, she was right. At that time (early 1990s), we still used hard paper rather than computer-generated receipts. Every January we received hundreds of calls from donors who could not find their receipts for income tax purposes. We filed the receipt numbers numerically to ensure that they were all accounted for. Once a series had been confirmed complete, I asked Alice to file them alphabetically so that when we received a call, we could easily find the receipt and photocopy it. This job kept Alice happy for well over 10 years until computers took over and Alice was sure that someone was sabotaging her work. I changed positions and moved from Vice-President of Regional Services at the Heart and Stroke Foundation to President and CEO of Easter Seals Ontario. Alice followed a few months later. She told me that the heart had gone out of the organization when I left, but I wasn't to tell her nephew.

When Sandra volunteered at Easter Seals, she worked under Alice's direction but found her to be a tough 'boss.'

As a volunteer, Alice was very demanding, but she demanded only what volunteers are entitled to expect— useful work, a comfortable designated space, free coffee, and recognition for a job well done. At the Heart and Stroke Foundation, Alice would drop the fact that Tony Graham was her nephew if she felt she needed a little clout. At Easter Seals she used my name because no one knew Tony. I smiled at her resourcefulness. Near the end of her tenure as a volunteer she ended up with her own office and name plate. Alice would become infuriated if anyone touched 'her stuff' between visits. Always dressed to the nines, she would come in with shoes matching her sweaters or purses in colors complementing the season. When winter came, I arranged for an underground parking spot because I worried about her slipping on the ice. I worried about her driving too, but that is another story. She asked me out for lunch one day and that started years of monthly lunches mostly in the building cafeteria, but a few times to an external restaurant. She always wished that she could find her way back to those restaurants to take her 'family' out. Alice had never married so her family in this instance was Dr. Tony Graham and his family. Alice insisted on paying every other month and so began our friendship.

We talked about the war, her job in the war, her career as a real estate agent, her family (siblings), how she got her dog from the market, her sister Sue's boys, and especially Tony, his wife Shannon, and their children because they lived closest. Then, we talked about my family, husband, children, and grandchildren. She would laugh and continue like a woman half her age and I always thought that I wanted to be just like her when I grew up! Her sense of independence and strength knew no age restriction.

I scolded her when she told me that during the Christmas season she drove into undesirable sections of the city and handed out $5.00 bills to the street people. She said that she stayed in the car and would only open the window enough to slide the bill out!

Our friendship really gelled after Barry and I remodelled our home. We were having some elderly neighbors in to see the results of the renovation and I asked if she would join us as well.

As always, Barry was the perfect host and asked all guests (5 women) if they wanted wine. Four said, "Yes." Alice said, "Rye, please, Crown Royal, on the rocks."

She won Barry's heart at once and she continued to flirt with him outrageously whenever we met. Barry's special story goes back to that same snowy evening when he walked Alice to her car so she would not fall. Barry was wearing cowboy boots and he slipped. Alice grabbed his arm and said, "Don't worry, honey. I've got you."

A few months later Alice reciprocated. Tony and Shannon made sure that the table was set for royalty, bringing dishes and utensils from their home to complement what Alice had. The five of us dined in splendor on Swiss Chalet Take-out as she beamed with pride.

The following Christmas brought tears to Alice's eyes. Tony's mom, her best friend and sister, was dying. I quickly put together an Advent Box with twenty-four individually wrapped little gifts, each marked with a December date. Alice and Sue talked every night and each day's gift became their topic of conversation. It made me happy to hear her laugh and see her wear the little green gloves with real bells for years afterwards.

When Sue died, the twinkle went out of Alice's eyes and the light went out of her heart. Alice was the last surviving member of her immediate family.

I will always think of her smiling, bold, and strong, a woman before her time asking me if my husband had a brother.

Chapter Seven

SHIFTING GEARS (YEARS 60-65)
2000-2005

I was not moving the organization in the merger direction that I wanted. My past training had been to move in, assess the situation, develop a plan, implement that plan and move out. The first three were easy, four and five were blocked by members of both organizations who preferred to maintain the status quo.

Barry's business had taken off and he wanted me to be available to travel with him whenever he could get away. My position was too senior to allow me to just drop everything and leave. At the time Easter Seals was a 30-million-dollar organization.

The icing on the cake came when our eldest son Brett announced that he and Sandra, his wife, were expecting their first child. We'd already welcomed our second grandson when Benjamin Joseph Clark came into our lives in 2003. A day or so after announcing that our daughter-in-law Sandra was pregnant, Brett called to say that they were having twins. We were ecstatic! Brett had always said that he was never getting married. Then he repeatedly told us that they were not having any children. Being the normal parents that we are, we said that we understood and grumbled behind their backs. We learned of Brett and Sandra's marriage a few years earlier when I came into the office and opened an email with the subject line reading, "Guess who got married on the weekend?" I scrolled down to the body of the email to see a picture of Sandra in a wedding dress and Brett in a tuxedo on the beach in the Bahamas. A few years later Sandra said they had eloped because they did not want all the family fuss. She said that she didn't even know where they were going until they were boarding the plane. She asked, "Why?"

Brett said that if his mom knew where they were getting married, she would be there. Sandra asked me, "You wouldn't. Would you?"

I said, "Yes, I would. I would have followed you to the moon and back. But that's just me."

I resigned from Easter Seals in January 2005 after the birth of the twins, but it took me nine months to ease out of the organization.

I retired and started a new career as a yoga instructor. We sold one home and bought three more properties, ending up with five properties in total (a townhouse in Waterloo, two in the North, one in Florida, and a 42-foot coach). My favorite three things became grandchildren, gardening, and the gym. Sandra came with me on several babysitting ventures. I smile remembering when four-year-old Ben taught her how to play a video game so that he would have a partner to beat.

This was the busiest decade of my life. My sister Sandra consumed the next four years. Christine and I searched for a safe place for her to live. Christine was stressed. Sandra was destroying her home. Christine's daughter Candy asked me to help. I told Candy that I had always been willing, but her mom consistently refused my help. Candy found a group home in the area, and I calmly moved Sandra from her room in Christine's house to a room in the group home. My life consisted of practicing yoga, teaching yoga, taking aquafit, gardening, and touching base with Sandra on a regular basis.

I took on a few consulting contracts, sat on two small volunteer boards and was on-call for 'grandma duty.' Barry and I travelled back and forth to the lake in the summer and took short weeklong trips in the winter when he was between contracts. I visited with Sandra regularly and eventually taught yoga at her long-term care facility. A few staff and of course Sandra participated. She laughed at the poses and positions that I asked her to hold. She loved when I arranged "theater nights" for a busload of residents to attend popular theater productions. My fundraising and donation background came in handy as I supported Sandra at this point in my life. When Sandra could no longer attend outside events, I stopped arranging the theater visits. One day when Sandra and I were having coffee in the lobby, a group of very able residents asked why there were no more theater outings. I was shocked and embarrassed that I had been so short-sighted. I immediately reached out to my contacts and the outings were reinstated.

Barry and I went looking for a trailer so that we could spend a few weeks of the year in Florida. We ended up buying a coach. We spent 3 weeks on a rental site in Naples, Florida and loved it. Barry was now winding down his business, so we booked 2-1/2 months for the following year. I never let Sandra consume my entire life. I had watched my Aunt Stella give up her life to take care of her daughter with Down's Syndrome. I knew that I needed to be balanced to be effective.

We had a dream, made it real, and moved forward. We decided to sell our beautiful home in Toronto and divide our time between three properties. We had our cottage in Barry's Bay, and we wanted a downsized property in Waterloo where the grandchildren lived. By now, we also knew that we wanted to own a property in Florida. I continued to sit on the Bendale Family Council, connecting by phone for regular monthly meetings. My sister Christine visited Sandra when she was able, and I supplemented the days that I could not visit with a paid sitter. Between Christine and I, we made sure that Sandra always had someone to visit with her. We knew the staff gave Sandra extra time and attention because they saw how attentive we were.

Not happy with letting our spanking new coach sit outside, Barry designed a garage to be built near our cottage on four acres of land. So now we had four properties to manage. I had shifted gears almost five years earlier, but Barry was busier than ever.

January, February, and March found us in Naples. June, July, and August found us at the lake. Christine, who had purchased a property in the same summer resort as us, also spent time at her cottage. We hired sitters to make sure that Sandra had at least one visitor who kept us informed of any changes in her health and happiness. Sandra may not have been 'balanced,' but she was being cared for. She broke a foot and seemed quite confused for a few months. A trip to the neurologist added an anti-seizure medication, which brought her back to us, humor and all. I was now chair of the Bendale Family Council, and Sandra received exceptional care. I often wondered if there was a connection.

We continued our 3-1/2 home lifestyle (Waterloo, Florida, lake, and garage) through the next several years. We added detours through Toronto after Barry's previously owned company went bankrupt. He started receiving calls directly from clients and chose to do major condo renovations. It suited me because it allowed for weekly lunches with Sandra. She loved hamburgers or fish and chips, so that became our once-a-week lunch menu. She loved hearing that Barry paid for the lunches! In her mind, when men paid, all was right with the world.

We were forced to pay a little closer attention to our own health in this decade. Barry continued to hunt, fish, maintain our four properties, and run a successful RV (recreational vehicle) show in Florida; all this and ten condo renovations in Toronto! I became a gym rat in Waterloo, taught yoga, and took water aerobics in Florida. I was the first Canadian and the first female president of the Pelican Lake Property Association in Florida and continued with Bendale activities in support of Sandra. It was about this time that I began to think about a direction for a book. Sandra was physically cared for but there was still something that did not seem right to me. I felt that there was more that Sandra and I could contribute to science and care.

It sounds like it was the best of times, but it was also the worst of times. Barry and I said our final farewells to Barry's mom, several friends, and our beautiful Doberman Spartacus. Sandra was devastated when one of her favorite support workers Flo died a year after our mom but on exactly the same day. It takes energy to grieve, and grieve we all did as we said our final goodbyes.

Bracken joined us the day after Spartacus died. Bracken is our sixth Doberman and our second red one. The plan was that Spartacus was to 'train' Bracken in the ways of being a good dog. We often think that Spartacus took one look at the puppy from across the river Styx in the kennel and said, "No way this 'bad boy' can be trained!" At ten years of age, Bracken still thinks he's boss!

I started my bucket list and arranged for our daughter, daughter-in-law, and grandchildren to join me on a Disney cruise. Christine joined us with her daughter and granddaughter. Barry continued to build, build, build.

With five children, there were always up' and downs, but as they aged, they continued to make us proud. Our grandchildren made us laugh, smile, and become their personal Uber drivers.

I spent 40 years believing that finding psychological balance was the key to our family's challenges. It would be years and many different experiences before I realized that my direction was wrong, but I always knew that Sandra's journey was her gift to me. It forced me to find balance as I continued to look for answers surrounding her challenges. Sandra motivated me to live the wonderful life that I continue to live and for that I am eternally grateful.

Chapter Eight

CHAOS AND ANARCHY (YEAR 66) 2006

"In the midst of chaos there is also opportunity."
(The Art of War)

Sandra started showing signs of declining function. She required a neurological assessment and a brain scan, but she had to see a psychiatrist and her family doctor needed to make the referral.

The week after we had been to the Center for Addiction and Mental Health (CAMH), Sandra and I went to see her family doctor. He had not received the report from CAMH. The attending doctor at the hospital had been busy but he promised that he would get right on it. Two weeks later I called the family doctor again. No report. He would not make the referral until he had received something in writing from CAMH. I called again and spoke with an assistant who was most helpful throughout the process. The attending doctor called and said that the report was being faxed to Sandra's family doctor. I called the family doctor who had left for a two-week vacation in Cuba. An appointment was made for Sandra for his first day in the office after his return. I had arranged to accompany her.

Knowing what was in the letter, I mentioned the need for Sandra to see a psychiatrist. I gave the family doctor the name and phone number of the psychiatrist closest to the group home where Sandra lived. I also asked about the brain scan and was told that Sandra should see the psychiatrist first. It was now March and Sandra, who had suffered from schizophrenic tendencies for over 30 years, had not seen a psychiatrist in over six months. She lost three metro passes, her teeth retainer, cigarettes, clothes, a lighter, and her glasses. Sandra was almost blind without her glasses. She was extremely frustrated and angry all the time. She accused the other residents of the group home with stealing and forcing her to go out and come home with money. I took Sandra home and discussed the situation with the house manager who set the record straight.

April 12th was Sandra's first psychiatric appointment. She went alone. There was neither a change in medication nor was there an appointment for a brain scan.

Sandra received a monthly government check under the Ontario Disability Support Program (ODSP). The check was meant to cover her living expenses and usually arrived on the last day of the month. Either Christine or I accompanied Sandra to the bank at the end of each month to try and get control of enough of her money to pay her expenses at the group home: room and board, cigarettes, and pocket change in case she wanted to buy pop, water, coffee, and a donut while she "tripped." Sandra called travelling on public transit "tripping."

It was now May. The beginning of cottage season. The end of the month fell on a Friday when both Christine and I were planning to be at the lake. Sandra told us that she had hired a lawyer because someone kept stealing her money from the bank. I wrote out an expense list and gave it to Sandra. I told her to have the teller put each amount in a separate envelope and give all the envelopes to Danny (manager of the group home). While we were away, Sandra gave Danny $300 and told him that she was moving to find a cheaper place. Both Christine and I returned from the lake and convinced Sandra to pay her bills. We relaxed for another month.

Numerous calls to the psychiatrist resulted in a June 28th appointment. Sandra was hostile and angry. She needed her medication increased. The psychiatrist made a note for the family doctor, advising him to increase Sandra's medication from 15mg to 20mg of Zyprexa (anti-psychotic medication) each evening and asked (in June!) if Sandra had seen a neurologist! He gave the note to Sandra to give to her family doctor. Sandra went to her family doctor's office. He was not working that day, so she left the note with the receptionist in a neighboring office! It was still difficult to totally take away Sandra's sense of independence.

Meanwhile, the end of June was approaching, and the last day again fell on a Friday. Both Christine and I had plans to be at the lake. We devised a plan. I went to the bank with Sandra and opened a 'joint account' telling Sandra that she would not have to pay daily transaction fees because I was over 60 years of age. Sandra visited each of her nine banks daily to withdraw or deposit loonies. All the tellers knew her. She was regularly thrown out of many financial institutions, but some treated her kindly and it was a place for her to go. By this time, Sandra was no longer capable of using the bank machine.

The plan was that Christine, who was not leaving until Friday morning, would go to the bank at 5:00 A.M. and withdraw the amount needed from the ATM before the bank opened at 8:00 A.M.

On June 29th at 5:00 A.M., Christine waited at the bank machine. She met Sandra there waiting for the bank to open. Christine inserted the card only to learn that Sandra had foiled us again. Sandra had a $500 daily limit and we needed $900. Christine took out the $500 and used the $385 from Sandra's income tax return plus $15 of her own money to pay Danny the required $900 for the month of July. The following day Christine tried to get the rest of the money out of an ATM (at the lake) but could only retrieve $200. Sandra had taken all but $217 out of her account.

Tuesday was my day to visit with Sandra. I returned from the lake to face problem number two. Sandra found her glasses, or someone in the group home found her glasses, but they only had one arm. I took Sandra to the optometrist where the glasses were purchased to see if they could replace the arm. They said that they have never been reimbursed for the glasses they made for Sandra in February. The glasses were expensive because of the heavy prescription. I asked if they could put a new arm on. Because Sandra broke the attachment area, a new arm was not a possibility. She needed a whole new frame. ODSP would not replace the frame in February because Sandra was only entitled to one new frame every two years, and she got new frames in 2006. The optometrist and I shared the cost of the frames in February. ODSP had agreed to pay for the lenses, which they did not.

The retiring owner of the optometry store asked if Sandra and I would accompany him to the ODSP office to clear up their lack of payment for the February prescription that they had approved. I cancelled the remainder of my commitments for the day and Sandra, the optometrist, and I went to the government office.

After an hour's wait, we were called. The new supervisor had no idea why the store was not reimbursed. She looked at Sandra's broken frames and approved payment for a new frame. In the car I asked the optometrist why they paid for replacement frames now when they refused in February.

The kind optometrist handed me the broken frames and said, "Keep these for whenever Sandra loses her glasses again. They need to see that they are broken." I tucked the glasses away and hoped that I never had to resort to lying in the future. But I knew that I would do whatever it took to get Sandra what she needed.

On Tuesday, July 10, I was feeling guilty having spent a wonderful week at the lake with my family (except Sandra). I called Sandra a few times to let her know that I was away and when I would be returning. I usually picked Sandra up around 9:15 A.M. but this morning I was there at 8:30 because often Sandra would leave right after breakfast and not return until the end of the day. Even when I tried to call the group home to see if Sandra was there, there would often be no answer or the answering machine would pick up. At 8:35, I went around to the back of the house to see if Sandra was outside smoking. One of the residents recognized me. Barry's company had paid for the whole house to go to Swiss Chalet for a Christmas dinner the previous year and they remembered. Nelida went into the house and got Sandra. Sandra came out furious, yelling and screaming that she hated living there and that she hated that man (Danny, the manager). Danny had not given her cigarette money for the day! I tried to calm her down, telling her that we were going to visit Christine and that she had cigarettes for her as well as a GST check.

Still furious, Sandra yelled, "If it's still there!"

Danny was using the cigarettes and coins to keep Sandra there until I arrived. It was a very clever strategy, and I made a mental note to get a nice dessert for everyone in the house to enjoy.

We went over to Christine's house, had a cup of tea, and picked up the GST check and a package of cigarettes.

I asked Sandra what she needed. She said, "Running shoes." She walked so much that she went through 2-3 pair of running shoes a year. The GST check was $90 and change. I said that if she kept $40, she could get some new running shoes and deposit $50 in the bank.

Flexing her independence, Sandra said "Maybe," and we left for the bank.

Sandra asked the teller to cash her check and deposit $10. The teller asked, "Which account?" I said that she only had one.

The teller corrected me and said that Sandra had two accounts; a checking account with $17 and a savings account with $180 (clever little woman). I smiled as Sandra tucked the money into her various shirt pockets. This was Sandra's strategy for not losing things. She had to wear a top with breast pockets or a zippered kangaroo pocket in the cooler weather. All her worldly necessities— metro pass, cigarettes, lighter, and coins— were in either her pockets or her sock!

We completed some errands that I had and went to Walmart for the running shoes. Sandra only took out the $40 that I had told her the shoes would cost. On the way from the parking lot, Sandra asked what would happen if the shoes cost more than $40. I reassured her that I would pay the difference. We were in luck. The running shoes were on special and only cost $25. Sandra put them on at once and she carried out the old shoes.

I asked Sandra if she needed anything else like socks or underwear. She said she needed underwear, white only and cotton. No one in the group home liked cotton so no one would steal them. We picked up a package of white cotton underwear and headed for the checkout. The total bill was $35. Sandra received $5 from the cashier which she added to her $40. She was elated. She had some new stuff, money in her pocket, and money in the bank. On the way out of the store Sandra dropped her old running shoes in the trash bin. Sandra now wanted to rid herself of my scrutiny and asked to be let off at the next corner. She had banking to do. We kissed, said good-bye, and agreed to meet the next Tuesday at 9:15 at the group home. We both left smiling.

The following Tuesday, I was again at the group home early, but I just waited in the car until Sandra appeared with her coins and her cigarettes. She came out wearing a sleeveless denim shirt with pockets on each breast, shorts, and a George Brown College 'wolf' cap. Christine worked at the college. Her teeth were stained, and her hair was long and scraggly. She looked like her hair needed a wash.

I looked at her at asked if she wanted her hair cut. She said yes and away we went. In the salon, while Sandra was in the back getting her hair shampooed, the other stylist asked if Sandra was my mother.

I said, "No, she is my sister."

"Is she your older sister?"

"No. She is seven years younger, but she has had a hard life."

I thought that Sandra might get a 'surf' cut like the one she had just outgrown, but she decided on a pixie cut which made her look like a boy, but that's what she wanted. Throughout the entire process, Sandra kept asking if her sister was still there because she had no money. I reassured her several times that I was still there. With her hair cleaned and styled, we both left the salon and headed off to the Farmer's Market, which is something I wanted to do. Sandra had had enough of me, even though it was only 11:00 A.M.

She asked me if she could take-off and trip from the market.

I said, "Sure."

Sandra kissed me good-bye and said, "I love you, Charlotte."

We both felt that we had had a good day.

Barry and I left for a weekend at the lake. I called Sandra several times. She was getting extremely agitated and angry. I called Sandra's family doctor from the lake. His receptionist answered. He is in the office Wednesdays, Thursdays, and Fridays. I told the receptionist that Sandra was getting worse. I needed to know if the doctor had increased her medication. I told her that it was my understanding that the psychiatrist had written to the family doctor and advised him to increase Sandra's medication.

The receptionist said that they had not seen Sandra in weeks. I explained that Sandra had dropped off the note from the psychiatrist at the neighboring medical office. She asked me to hold. She went to the next office, retrieved the note, and read it to me (against all privacy legislation, but bless her; she received an arrangement of flowers from me the following week to thank her for all her assistance).

Sandra's psychiatrist did indeed request that Sandra's family doctor increase her Zyprexa from 15 to 20mg. As a result of our January visit to CAMH, he also asked if Sandra had seen a neurologist. It was now July.

The receptionist repeated that Sandra had not been in to get a revised prescription and she said that she would have to contact the psychiatrist's office to see if they had booked a neurological assessment. I said that a neurological assessment had not been booked. I explained that the family doctor would have to direct him to do so. I asked if Sandra could have a doctor's appointment on

Thursday, July 19. I told her that I would accompany Sandra. The appointment was made for 10:30 A.M.

Sandra was thrilled. Two visits in one week. I picked her up and was early again. Sandra had me conditioned. This time, Sandra came out and gestured for me to wait a few minutes until she got her coins and cigarettes. Sandra was wearing the same blue denim shirt with the double-breasted pockets, a pair of denim jeans and the same baseball cap. We had tea at Christine's house. Sandra had instant coffee. At 9:45 Sandra and I left for the doctor's office. I told Sandra that I had also arranged for her to see a foot doctor in the afternoon. Sandra's toenails were grossly deformed and thick. The only appointment I could get was at 4:30. After her morning appointment, I thought that Sandra could 'trip' and go off on her own for a few hours. I told her that she must be at the group home at 4:00 P.M. so that we could go to the foot doctor. Sandra heard that the appointment was at 4:00 P.M. and I didn't correct her. I wanted to make sure that she showed up. Christine advised me to keep Sandra with me all day long, an impossible task, to make sure that she turned up for the later appointment. Sandra said that she understood. She told us that she was not a baby. She asked me to meet her at the Tim Horton's beside the foot doctor's office so that she would not have to go back to the group home until after all her appointments were over. We agreed.

When Sandra and I arrived at the family doctor's office in the morning, the receptionist handed me the file and said that we could go right in. The letter that the receptionist and I discussed was right on top.

The doctor's office was divided into three areas — an examination area which was behind him, his desk area which he filled by being an exceptionally large man, and the patient area consisting of two big leather chairs in front of his desk. Connecting the doctor and patient area were shelves filled with model cars. I assumed that this was a hobby of his. Given that Sandra was the patient, I directed her to the first seat, and I took the second.

My first bad move was to speak before Sandra spoke and say that we were there to get a prescription increase. The doctor spoke only to Sandra and ignored me. He shuffled through the files and noted that Sandra had seen the psychiatrist on April 12th and that she was on thyroid medication and Zyprexa 15mg. He asked Sandra how she liked the new psychiatrist. Sandra said that he only spoke to her for two minutes and then said goodbye. She commented that she preferred her previous psychiatrist. She asked her family doctor if he had ever met her previous psychiatrist.

He said, "No."

This appointment was not going well at all. Sandra was sounding very lucid. I had called from the lake after hearing that the psychiatrist was recommending a 5mg increase in Zyprexa for Sandra.

I had asked Danny if he had any extra Zyprexa on hand. He said yes and said that he would give Sandra an extra 5 mg a day. I reassured him that I would get a prescription from the family doctor the following Thursday. Danny had started Sandra on the increased dosage a week before her doctor's appointment.

By the time that the family doctor saw Sandra, she had been taking the increased dosage for over a week. It was doing its job. She was calm, still forgetful, but lucid. I did not want to get the receptionist in trouble for breaching privacy laws, but the family doctor had obviously not read his notes carefully. The receptionist told me that the letter from the psychiatrist was right on top.

I spoke again calmly and quietly and said that I was sure that Sandra had seen her psychiatrist at the end of June, and that he had sent a letter right away. I asked the family doctor if he had received it. He shuffled through the many papers in her file and finally said that he had it. Sandra had seen her psychiatrist on June 28[th,] and he had advised an increase in Zyprexa to 20mg. He asked Sandra if she needed anything else. She said Tylenol 3 for her arthritis, which he prescribed, more thyroid medication, which if he had looked in his files, he would have seen that she had more than a year's worth of repeats.

She thought that she needed allergy medication because it's allergies that make her go crazy in the spring and the fall. He said that the allergy medication was not covered but that he would prescribe it for her. He also asked her (finally, he was with the program) if she had seen a neurologist.

She looked at him sideways and I answered, "No."

He said that the offices were 'way' downtown on Sherbourne Street. I said that I would take her. He said that it would be a two to three month wait. I said that was fine. The doctor made a note to have the receptionist make the arrangements. I made a note to follow up in two weeks if I had not heard anything.

He commented that Sandra had ten repeats for the Zyprexa so she would not have to come in for a while. He said that her blood pressure had always been fine, but he didn't take it. He asked if she had any other problems. Sandra commented about her toes. I said that we were seeing a chiropodist that afternoon.

We left the office, Sandra smiling and me biting my tongue. We kissed and agreed to meet at 4:00 P.M. at Tim Horton's. Sandra boarded public transportation to 'trip' for a few hours.

At 3:35 P.M., I was at the Tim Horton's having coffee. Sandra was nowhere to be seen. I watched as crowds streamed out of the buses, but no Sandra. At 3:55 P.M., I called Danny to see if Sandra had returned to the group home. She was not there. I walked across to the chiropodist's office and explained that Sandra would not make her appointment. I added that I would have to call in September because I was seldom in the city on a Thursday. I went back to the donut shop and bought a dozen donuts as treats for the residents of the group home when they took their evening medication at 7:00 P.M. While driving up the street, my phone rang.

It was Danny. Sandra was at the house. I parked in the driveway, handed Danny the donuts, and held the car door open for Sandra to get in. On the way back down the street, I reminded Sandra that we had agreed to meet at the Tim Horton's at 4:00 P.M. to see the foot doctor. Sandra simply said that she had forgotten.

The chiropodist was extremely kind and very patient. Sandra's feet were dirty (of course), and we were late (of course). I knew that there was a $40 consultation fee, but I was going to try and talk him out of it.

One look at Sandra's feet and he said that in his 25 years of practice, he had only seen one patient with feet as bad as Sandra's and that individual only had the deformity in one foot. Sandra had it in both feet.

She suffered from an extremely high instep, so high that it caused her feet to turn to the outside. Sandra walked on the sides of her feet rather than the bottoms. He said that he was surprised that she had not broken ankles and legs over the years.

Both Sandra and I confirmed that as a child Sandra was always breaking something. As an adult she suffered a severe ankle break which necessitated a plate and screws being inserted into her ankle. He cut and ground her nails down as far as he could on one visit and checked 'chiropody treatment' on the receipt, telling me to try and get ODSP to pay. He wanted to see Sandra again at no charge to see what he could do for her feet.

I drove Sandra quickly back to the group home so that she would not miss supper. We kissed, smiled, and agreed to meet the following Tuesday.

We struggled through the next several months. Sandra had her brain scan and saw a neurologist who confirmed the diagnosis of 'dementia.'

Then, one Friday night in November, Sandra never returned to the group home after tripping. Danny called me, and I called Christine to see if Sandra was there. No one had seen her.

We called the police and everyone we knew who Sandra may have visited. No luck. No Sandra. My husband and I had booked a trip to Cuba, leaving the following Wednesday. We were ready to cancel on Monday when I received a call from a social worker in Etobicoke, the west end of Toronto. Sandra was totally unfamiliar with that part of the city. The social worker, bless her, had looked at all the housing applications and found one from three years prior listing me as the contact person. Sandra was in hospital, confused, and with a broken wrist. She was found in a snowbank, hurt and disoriented. The police took her to the nearest hospital.

That November day had been extremely cold, and by the time Sandra walked to the subway and started to ride, she fell asleep. The subway went to the far end of the line when they asked all passengers to disembark. Sandra got off in an area totally foreign to her. She went outside, fell, and couldn't get up. She lay there until someone called the police. With nothing familiar, she became frightened and disoriented. The hospital staff thought that she was speaking gibberish. I could have interpreted, but then I was not there. She was alone. She could have died. She was only 53 years old.

We found out later that the group home insisted that all residents leave the house for a few hours every day so that they could clean. Some residents had programs that they could attend. Some had little part-time jobs. Some just visited friends or relatives. Neither Christine nor I were aware of this rule. Sandra had no program or little job to go to. I tried to link her with services or programming on several occasions. Christine and I weren't always available.

I called the Salvation Army Transitional Employment Program to ask about Sandra joining the program. I asked if they had received everything and if all the paperwork was complete. I was told that they had all they needed.

Sandra could start the recreational program immediately, but there was a waiting list for the work program. Sandra was number eight on the waiting list and it could be anywhere from a few weeks to a few months. They felt that a few months was the more realistic timeline.

Sandra called from the group home and asked me if I was coming to visit her the following day, a Tuesday.

I said, "Yes," and that I hoped that she would be there.

She knew that I was angry because I had driven all the way over there twice in the last week and she had taken off before I got there. She offered to buy me a coffee. I said that would be nice.

Sandra never attended the Recreational Program at the Salvation Army. She did have a few friends, plus Christine and me. Everyone was busy with their own lives and, while we did give Sandra whatever time we had, it was never enough. She would trip to her many banks or ride the subway for hours to fill time.

The next three months, finding a safe place for Sandra to live became a 24/7 job for me. I was retired from my position as President and CEO of the Easter Seals Society of Ontario. If I had not been retired, I never would have had the time or energy to provide the support that Sandra required.

First, I needed to have Sandra declared 'incompetent,' which was no easy task. Sandra was brilliant and could outwit many of the overworked doctors and medical personnel who tried to provide support for her.

I accompanied her to the psychiatrist's office. As we sat in the waiting room, I could hear her asking other patients what day it was and what was happening in the world so that she could continue an intelligent conversation when she was talking with the doctor. I had to think of a way to get around this roadblock. I wasn't allowed into the office with Sandra, but I knew what her triggers were. I decided to write to her psychiatrist and provide him with a list of triggers that would set Sandra off.

At her next appointment, Sandra's doctor asked Sandra if I could sit in on her meeting if I didn't speak. Sandra agreed. I believe that her psychiatrist wanted me to see how lucid Sandra was.

They had their friendly interaction and spoke about her medication and any challenges she might be having. She said that she did not like where she was living.

He only got to ask my first suggested trigger.

"Who pays your rent?" he asked.

Sandra started screaming and yelling that she was sponsored and people were stealing her money.

His eyes turned into saucers when she put her fist through the wall. I calmed her down. He looked at me and said that we would speak later.

The date was December 17, 2007. He called that evening and said that Sandra needed to be admitted to a hospital for assessment and relocation into a long-term care facility. I asked if it could be after Christmas and he said no. There were currently no beds available and there would be no beds available after Christmas. Everyone wanted their loved one home for Christmas, but then they would quickly readmit them once the holiday season was over. It was now or never. Much to my family's disappointment, I agreed. Sandra was admitted to hospital on December 20th, 2007.

Sandra was diagnosed as incompetent on December 24th, 2007. Sandra was still a smoker at this time and needed to exit the hospital to smoke. Christine and I took turns visiting daily to take her out. I sat in my car and cried after my December 21st visit. When I went up to her floor, Sandra was bruised and limping. She said that she was fine. She just had to learn the rules. She had sat in another patient's chair at mealtime and when the occupant of the chair came to have her meal, she knocked Sandra on the floor as her way of introducing her to the 'rules.'

I was upset but the incident reminded me of two previous times when Sandra tried to protect me from the harsh realities of her life. Once when I was still living in Toronto, Sandra came to me and asked if I thought she needed to 'go in.'

She was hallucinating and I said, "Yes."

She said, "OK."

I drove her to CAMH, called 999 Queen Street at the time, and went to get out of the car. Sandra said, "No. I do not want you to see the inside of this building. I will not go in if you accompany me."

I said okay and drove away crying.

The second time, I was living up north with my family and Sandra hitchhiked all the way up and asked if I thought she needed to be admitted. She did. She was hallucinating again, but this time I was working for a doctor and had heard of Homewood, a wonderful place in Guelph that had a bowling alley, a hairdressing salon, and little cafes. I arranged for Sandra to be admitted.

When I drove her down, we toured the facility and then I walked with her to a large metal door. The door opened automatically. Sandra went in with an orderly who told me that I wasn't allowed to go any further. When the door clanged shut and locked, I slumped to the floor and cried.

I shared this incident with Sandra several years later and told her how I had felt and how I had never forgotten that feeling of her being locked away from me. She smiled and said that when she heard the door lock, she thought she could relax because she was safe now.

It would be many years in the future when Sandra would again amaze me. She had been in the long-term care facility for several years. She contracted a virus and was hooked up to oxygen and intravenous antibiotics. When I saw her, the tears automatically started rolling down my cheeks. She looked at me with questions in her eyes.

I said, "It's nothing. I just don't like seeing all those tubes and oxygen going into your body."

Still as strong as an ox, Sandra started pulling everything out so I would not be upset. I stopped her, laughed, and thought what an amazing woman she was.

Chapter Nine

WHERE DOES SANDRA BELONG?
(YEAR 66-67) 2007-2008

Few people are aware of what an ordeal the administrative process can be. As past President and CEO of The Easter Seal Society of Ontario, I was aware of how cumbersome government administrative processes could be. I knew how much advocating would be required to support Sandra and I was up for the challenge.

Christine and I knew that Bendale Acres Long Term Care facility was the best location for Sandra. It was within walking distance of Christine's house, and because I lived in Waterloo (100 km away) and travelled a lot, we wanted to make visiting Sandra as easy as possible for Christine. Christine said that she wanted me to manage anything administrative and financial, and she would visit. I visited as well, but not as much as Christine.

I familiarized myself with the guidelines and questions to ask when choosing a long-term care facility (provided by the Province of Ontario in 2007).

On Monday (first Monday in January 2008), I called Stephanie, the social worker who I had been working with at the hospital to make sure that I was aware of all the questions to ask.

I called Bendale Acres to ask whether they used wrist guards and/or alarms to ensure that residents didn't get lost. I also wanted to know whether they accepted smokers and whether they had a secure smoking area. I didn't like Sandra smoking, but it was her only pleasure, and if something were available, it would be worth it. I learned that there was a waiting list for a basic room at Bendale Acres, but I didn't know how long the list was.

- Leisure World on Ellesmere had a one year waiting list.
- Leisure World in Scarborough also had a waiting list.
- Providence Villa did have wander guards but absolutely no smoking.
- True Davidson Acres Long Term Care facility had wander guards, a secure outdoor wandering area, and a 3– to 6–month waiting list.

I received a form from the Community Care Access Centre (CCAC) advising me to apply for all pension supplements that Sandra would be entitled to. At this point in time, Sandra was only 56 years old. I was continually telling people that Sandra was my sister and not my mother.

I spoke with Sandra's Public Guardian, who advised me to follow up with the Ontario Disability Support Program (ODSP) to get Sandra's T4 for her 2007 Income Tax. At first, I thought what a wonderful service this Public Guardian provided. She was there to answer my questions. It was not long before I realized that she, or the government — I'm not sure which — charged Sandra $20 a month to advise me how to function. All the actual work was left for me.

In order to take care of Sandra, I needed to fill in numerous government forms and supply supporting documentation to gain power of attorney over her affairs.

I called my local CCAC to ask if they had the forms to apply for any income supplements. I was told that the paperwork would be given to us once Sandra had been accepted at a facility. The facility would then apply.

I learned that I must choose three facilities. Only one could have a long waiting list. That one was, of course, our number one choice — Bendale Acres. The other two were to be chosen from a place with a short waiting list, a list that CCAC provided. I chose two from that list. Before I was able to arrange my tours, one facility refused Sandra admission.

All ODSP payments plus any supplements would go to pay for Sandra's accommodation. There would be $120 stipend a month for clothing, toiletries, hair care, nail care, and pocket change.

My husband and I had plans to visit Florida for seven to ten days. I needed a break. I had chosen three sites and left my contact information in Florida with the hospital. The hospital did call a few times while I was in Florida. I told them that Christine could oversee the move from hospital to a long-term care facility when the call came. At this time, I had received no correspondence from the any of the sites chosen.

Christine was concerned that the hospital would put pressure on her to take Sandra into her home. She was upset and said that could not manage having Sandra in her house. She would have to stay up until 10 P.M. to give Sandra her nightly medication. She was not physically able do it. I told Christine that she was not to discharge Sandra under any circumstances. She would lose her bed in the hospital and there would be no pressure for them to continue to collaborate with me to find Sandra an appropriate placement. I told her to give them my return date and say that I would contact them upon my return.

The hospital did call Christine while I was away and told her that there was an outbreak on Sandra's floor. She was asked if she could take Sandra home for the weekend. She did take her home for the weekend but would not discharge her. She was threatened with a move for Sandra to Whitby Psychiatric Hospital. Whitby was over an hour's drive from Toronto (where Christine lived) and two hours from Waterloo (where I lived). Sandra also didn't need a psychiatric hospital placement. She needed long term care.

Upon my return, I commented that it would be a big mistake to move Sandra to Whitby, and I was going to take some political and media action. I wanted her assessment redone. The assessment was the problem, not Sandra.

On January 28th I received an email from Sandra's Mental Health Therapist (a social worker named Stephanie). She had been in contact with the CCAC. There were four homes currently on the short list that the CCAC thought were appropriate for Sandra: Fudger House, Castleview Wychwood, Heritage Place and Craiglee, which was very dirty, but this was also sixteen years ago. I noted that no one considered distance from relatives for visiting purposes when they considered placements.

An additional three considerations were Main Street Versa Care, which was currently not on the short list; Trilogy, which had seventy-two females on the wait list; and Wexford Place, which I could not tour because they currently had an infectious outbreak. Their wait list was six months plus. I knew that the hospital wanted Sandra discharged and would not consider a six month wait.

In her first week in hospital, Sandra, a smoker, followed a patient off the ward to have a cigarette. She was located when she was trying to find her way back. It was documented in her chart that she was trying to escape.

A social worker from the CCAC (Community Care Access Center) used a Residential Assessment Interview (RAI) form to determine Sandra's eligibility for placement in a long-term care facility in January 2008. I asked her to document the fact that Sandra was trying to find her way back to the ward and not trying to escape. Shortly after, I learned the term 'exit seeking.' Sandra was not exit seeking, but I was continually told that CCAC was looking for a locked ward.

A very formal letter dated January 25, 2008, stated that True Davidson Acres had received the application for Sandra Wengle, and they were sorry, but they were unable to accept the application.

Their staff lacked the nursing expertise necessary to meet her needs. They thanked me for my interest in their center.

They suggested that I continue to collaborate with the Community Care Access Center Placement Services to obtain a placement that would best meet our needs. They copied the CCAC Coordinator and the Compliance Advisor, both were different individuals than those copied on the first declining letter. I called CCAC directly and asked why Sandra was denied admission. I was told that it was because she smoked. By this time Christine and I had turned Sandra into a non-smoker. They continued to look for a locked ward.

Stephanie informed me that they did an updated behavioral assessment, and that Sandra was down to one cigarette a day. Leisure World Ellesmere may reconsider. Bendale still had not responded. I was told that Sandra was becoming less preoccupied with smoking. If Christine and I did not visit, Sandra didn't make a big deal about not being able to go out. If Sandra quit smoking completely, they would update the behavioral assessment. Stephanie advised that we select an additional two or three back-up choices.

On January 29th, 2008, there was still no response from Bendale Acres. There were still thirty-nine individuals ahead of Sandra on the waiting list. Leisure World was reviewing, and a behavioral reassessment was requested.

I wondered what individuals would do if they had no advocate. I found out when touring one facility with my husband. My heart went out to a woman in her eighties who Barry described as 'not knowing the difference between bacon and eggs' actively searching for a placement for herself.

Sandra loved it in the hospital. She felt safe. We felt that she would learn to love living in a long-term care facility.

My second choice for a nursing home denied Sandra's application. The rejection letter went to the Public Guardian who said that she should never have received it. I informed both the social worker at the hospital and the case worker at CCAC. They sent me a copy of the letter. I never did receive anything notifying me of the second rejection.

I asked why Sandra was rejected:

- Because she smoked (I told everyone we met that she no longer smoked)
- Because she wandered (I added that she was not exit seeking; she got lost)

I was then told that they did not have the staff to accommodate her needs. Neither decision maker knew that Sandra no longer smoked or that she was never exit-seeking.

By this time, I realized the urgency of becoming Sandra's guardian. I worked full-time for the next two months trying to gain guardianship and find a facility appropriate for Sandra.

The psychiatrist and social worker requested a meeting on Friday, February 1st at 10:30. The psychiatrist asked if I knew the reason for the meeting. I said that I assumed that it was an update. He told me that it was an update among other things.

We discussed Sandra's progress, and I thanked him for her improved behavior on medication. I stated that her dementia had not improved. He commented that her schizophrenia (paranoia) would continue to improve slowly over time, but her dementia would increase. We both agreed that she required the assisted care and supervision that a long-term care facility was able to provide.

He asked if I knew how expensive it was to keep Sandra in hospital now that she was stable. I asked what he wanted me to do. He said that I must choose nursing homes that might not be as desirable, at least until our number one choice had space.

He mentioned some nice nursing homes, and I told him that I was not allowed to choose from that list. He looked at the social worker and she confirmed. I informed him that no nursing home had accepted Sandra's application to date, but that I was continuing to tour.

He asked why, and I told him that it was about smoking, which was no longer an issue, and wandering, which had never been an issue. He said that was ridiculous. Sandra was fully clothed with shoes and could leave at any time. I told him that I had requested a reassessment several times over the past few weeks. He looked to the social worker, who confirmed my comment and said that the assessor was sick last week and that she was currently on personal leave.

On February 5th, I spoke with the social worker. She confirmed that both Wexford and Fudger House could be on Sandra's short list after Bendale Acres.

I asked when the reassessment was being scheduled. The social worker was not sure, but she said that she would follow up.

I told her that Sandra may say that she is a smoker, but all anyone needed to do was to look at the 'in/out' book and see that she hadn't been out in over a week.

Wexford only had two on the waiting list but was currently closed to the public due to an outbreak.

Stephanie confirmed that if Sandra went to Fudger House, it would only be until a place became available at Bendale Acres, our first choice.

On February 8, 2008, I called Wexford Place to book a tour the following Tuesday. The tour was cancelled because of a 'Militant Uprising.'

I wondered but never found out what that was about.

I spoke with the social worker at the hospital regarding the scheduling of the reassessment. The assessor was still on personal leave. She commented that there were outbreaks of illness everywhere and some beds should be opening soon.

On February 11, 2008, I called the hospital again to speak with the social worker. I wanted to confirm which homes were on Sandra's short list and ask about the reassessment. (RAI)

I had listed four concerns that the assessor may have:

- Sandra had been diagnosed as having schizophrenic tendencies (they were controlled by medication).
- She was listed on the first assessment as being 'exit seeking' (not true).
- Sandra was a smoker (3 weeks without a cigarette).
- Incontinent (never).

I called the Public Guardian and asked if she could access a copy of the RAI assessment.

When I met with the Executive Director of the East York CCAC, she said that I should be talking to the Central East CCAC because that is where Sandra lived. She gave me a name to call and mentioned that she was on the advisory board of True Davidson Acres and that there was a waiting list of seventy-six applicants.

I called the Central East CCAC and explained the situation with the assessment. The person who answered said that she would investigate. She left me a message later that day to say that she had followed up with the case manager at the hospital who would follow up with the social worker. Once she heard anything, she would call me back. No call backs.

On February 19, 2008, I was told that there were two on the waiting list at Bendale Acres for a semi ($1700/month). I was also informed that basic accommodation is 100 percent covered by ODSP and that Sandra could not afford a semi.

The public guardian also confirmed that she would return Sandra's birth certificate, expired passport, and health card needed to transfer power of attorney over to me.

I insisted that my sister, Christine, also be listed as having power of attorney. Christine said no, and we argued. I pointed out that I was 5 years older than her and if anything should happen to me, I didn't want her to have all the hassle of applying. She reluctantly agreed, but again reaffirmed that she only wanted to visit Sandra and have nothing to do with administration. I reassured her that I would take on that responsibility and visit whenever I could.

I also learned that 'semi' is 'basic' and is covered by ODSP. I wondered who knew what in the whole scheme of things.

On February 21st, I received an email from the social worker at the hospital informing me that there were still no nursing homes on the short wait list. She suggested I tour Tony Stacey Center (fabulous staff), Thompson House (incredibly old, no), Altamont, Extendicare, Scarborough (no), and Rockcliff (no). She again mentioned that Wexford could be a possibility and they would like at least one more choice sent to the CCAC by the middle of the following week. There was still no answer from Bendale Acres.

On February 27, 2008, I picked Sandra up from the hospital at 8:00 A.M. I had arranged a tour of two homes, and I had planned a drop-in at Bendale just to see if it was worthy of a tour.

Between nine and ten in the morning, we toured Wexford Place. Sandra liked it. It was clean and residents seemed happy. I liked the internet café and thought that Christine would enjoy the monthly bus tours to Casino Rama. It would be something that she could do with Sandra. Wexford Place is run by a religious group. They are a non-profit organization and fundraise for any extras.

Sandra and I went to Bendale at 10:30 and I asked to speak with the administrator. I was told that she was on a half hour break and that I was to call the CCAC. I said that this was not a CCAC problem. I told them that Sandra's application went into Bendale on January 8th. Provincial legislation states that they have five days to respond. As of February 27, I had received no response. The CCAC had received no response.

I asked to speak with the administrator's supervisor.

A junior co-ordinator came out of the business area. I explained our concern. She invited us into the office area. She looked on her desk and then a second desk. She went to the back-window area where she looked through a pile of papers. These are my thoughts only, but the pile of papers looked like the "problem file."

The co-ordinator said that they still had some questions. The admissions committee was meeting at that very moment, and she assured me that they would review the application. I said that I was there and would answer any questions they had.

I said that an incorrect assessment was originally sent. She agreed and said that a second assessment had been forwarded, but they still had some behavioral issues that needed to be addressed.

At 2:00 P.M., Sandra and I toured True Davidson Acres. Sandra was exhausted. She kept sitting down and not paying attention.

Sandra's overall comment on the day was that she was comfortable that wherever she went would be a nice place.

On February 28th, I received a letter from True Davidson Acres. They were unable to approve the application because they did not have the specialized staffing resources required to meet Sandra's needs.

Sandra was admitted to the psychiatric wing of a hospital on December 20, 2007. Her status as incompetent came on December 24, 2007. She was transferred to Bendale Acres on March 7, 2008.

We were told at the first Family Consult meeting that having had Sandra assessed, and with the extent of her dementia, she could be with us for three more years. Sandra died July 23, 2019, eleven and half years after her admission.

95

Chapter Ten

THE PHYSICAL SIDE OF BALANCE (YEARS 69-76) 2009-2019

To quote Sir Winston Churchill, "A positive thinker sees the invisible, feels the intangible and achieves the impossible."

My focus was still Sandra, but I was wearing down. I needed to rejuvenate. I needed to rediscover what made me feel good; what made me feel strong, and what kept me positive. I started with yoga.

I took Hatha yoga classes for about ten years. I was still working and over the years discovered other strategies that would keep me feeling good and moving forward. By this time, I acknowledged that the key to curing or even just helping Sandra wasn't just having her find a sense of balance. There was something else; something I was missing. I was committed to supporting Sandra as best I could, while maintaining my own sense of balance while I continued my search.

I loved yoga, the way it made me feel, and the way I could move gave me a sense of presence when I walked into a room. I was calm, confident, and in control.

I discovered both my body and my mind on a two-by-six-foot mat. The moves encouraged me to explore my whole being and allowed me to listen to my body. That key learning would save my life in future years.

It was an escape to lie back, close my eyes, clear my mind, and focus on being totally in the space where I was lying.

Contrary to what most people believe, yoga is not just a set of exercises or meditative techniques. The exercises and techniques are aids meant to lead you to a state of mind. That state of mind can lead you through those times in life when you are faced with extreme difficulties or challenged with severe pain. It is one of the reasons that the U.S. Army introduced yoga and especially breathing and meditation into the training of their soldiers. They hope not only to increase the efficacy of their soldiers but also to reduce the number returning with PTSD.

I learned how to direct my mind exclusively toward an object and sustain that direction without distraction. There is an inversion exercise where I would lie down on my back and extend my arms and legs to the ceiling. I learned to focus either on the music or my breath as a single point of focus. It sounds simple, even relaxing, and it was suggested that we only hold the position for one to three minutes. I became the center of attention when football and hockey players taking the class collapsed their extensions after three minutes and I held my position for fifteen. It took practice and I'm sure that I couldn't do it now, but I know that I would still be able outlast many.

In his book, *The Ravenous Brain*, Daniel Bor (2012) explains how the brain and the mind are two separate entities. One cannot survive without the other. The goal is to cross the mind/body or mind/brain divide. I learned to clear my mind and focus on being in the space of my practice.

The breath is the best tool to deepen concentration. I learned to breathe deeply and rhythmically and visualize my breath. As I inhaled through my nose, I mentally followed my breath as it flowed down my spinal column around the base of my spine, up the other side and out. As I exhaled, I thought about the stale oxygen and negative energy winding up the opposite side of my spine and out. Each inhale I drew allowed fresh oxygen and positive energy to fill my entire body. A full exhale emptied my lungs allowing me to inhale this revitalizing force. I became one with my breath.

Yoga exercises may look like body contortions, but when you learn the rationale behind the position, you can appreciate and understand the outcome.

I needed to focus on taking care of myself so I could take care of others. In my professional capacity, my speeches often included comments about how continued stress will wear a person down and leave one susceptible to disease and illness.

When I was in my early twenties, I remember drawing a picture of myself walking out of the water on a beach. People were hanging from my body everywhere like bloodsuckers. I had no desire to remove any of them. I could identify each one of them, and they were all important to me, my nuclear family, my extended family, and those who became family by choice rather than by blood.

I needed to be strong. I couldn't help anyone if I couldn't function. I would burn out. I set aside time each day for a physical activity to keep my body strong.

As the years went by and life threw lemons at me in the form of illness, death of those close to me, and a pandemic, I was forced to modify my activities. I never thought of eliminating any of them. I kept moving! When I was young, swimming was my activity of choice. I swam and swam and, as previously mentioned, dated lifeguards along the way. When I moved from one decade to the next, I moved to aquafit classes and yoga. Yoga became my passion, leading me to become an instructor. Throughout my life, walking has been an activity that allows me think and dream, as well as move. Upon retiring, I became a gym rat. I was addicted to a weightlifting class. After several years of weightlifting, I noticed some black floaters in my left eye. I was halfway through a class when they first appeared. I focused on those floaters and studied what was happening to me. I closed my left eye, no floaters. I closed my right eye, floaters. I thought that I should get my eyes checked out. I went from doctor to eye surgeon in the same day and learned that my left retina had detached slightly from my optic nerve, and I needed rest. If rest did not solve the problem, I would need surgery. That was the end of the weightlifting class but not the end of the gym.

Six weeks later found me in a "Fit Fix" class which I religiously attended every morning. After three years of classes, I was finding some of the movements difficult. I would tire and my arms didn't seem strong enough to hold my body in a plank position. I'd always considered age a number, not a condition. I moved to a fitness regimen that I thought might be easier. Body Flow, a combination of yoga and Pilates became my class of choice until the pandemic shut me down. I modified my movements, but I never stopped moving.

When I became ill, walking and a few yoga movements replaced the structured gym classes. I bought a Fitbit and started logging 1,000 steps a day. I knew that the goal was 10,000 steps, but I also knew that was beyond my capability at that point in my recovery. I did what I could, but I continued to move. I also put "walk" as my number one item on my to do list every day. Movement continues to be a priority for me.

Every day I set aside time for a physical activity that I enjoyed. I loved to physically check off that I had completed my goal no matter how small the goal had become. Sandra had walked for miles every day. When she couldn't walk any longer, Christine or I would push her in a wheelchair. She wanted the sun on her face and the wind in her hair. It made her feel alive.

Along the same lines, I set a goal of cleaning one thing, one room, one drawer, one bed each day. Cleaning added to my Fitbit steps, kept our living space clean and made me smile with a sense of accomplishment. I used to try and clean the whole house in one day and then do no housework for the rest of the week. I learned to do my physical activity of choice first, and then to do one household activity to make our surroundings a place to enjoy.

Was I perfect? No. Did I have all the answers? No. I did what kept me going and kept me strong. I am ashamed to say that when Sandra died, I went through her drawers and closet and ended up with five large garbage bags of old clothes, birthday cards from years past, bags with hard food items still in them, and dust to fill a vacuum cleaner twice over. Why didn't I think of going through her drawers sooner? When I saw her PSWs struggling to put a bra on her every day, I thought, "For Heaven's sake." I find my bra restrictive at the end of each day. At that time, I went through her drawers, threw out all the bras and bought her tank tops to wear under her sweaters or blouses. They kept her warm and looking presentable. I don't know why I never thought of going through all her drawers and cupboards on a regular basis. I don't know who I thought would clean the closet and drawers. She had jeans and tops to accommodate fluctuating weight changes. There was no room for any more clothes, but we continued to buy her new items for Christmas and birthdays for each of those eleven years that she resided at Bendale Acres.

In December 2020, I noticed that some of my adult friends were fading from the restrictions of the pandemic. I also noticed that my husband was stressed with all the stuff we had to get rid of once the pandemic was over and we were planning to downsize from two homes to one. I sent out an email to two friends, included my husband, and copied myself. I said that we were going to do a 'reverse advent donation' for each day during the month of December. Each day I sent out a motivational declutter quote. One day they received Albert Einstein's quote, "Out of clutter, find simplicity, from discord, find harmony, in the middle of difficulties lies opportunity."

The first day my husband gave me a broken pencil. I thought, "This isn't going very well at all." He said that he loved all his stuff.

Barry was hooked when he found out that he could actually sell some of our unused stuff and make money.

Pandemic or no pandemic, I had always loved staying connected. I was often described as a 'collector of people.' I loved people. However, I must admit that I almost became overwhelmed with the number of email jokes and texts that I received over the pandemic years. It took me away from working on my manuscript, delaying my writing for weeks at a time. I learned to set aside a certain amount of time each day to stay connected either by forwarding emails, responding to emails, sending birthday cards, or writing notes.

Before she died, Sandra tried to mimic my behavior. I have a box of her cards, limericks, journal writings, and pictures. Everyone needs to feel that they belong somewhere. The only difference between Sandra and I was that I sent them out to others, and after a short while, Sandra only sent them to me or put them in a box. At this time Sandra was not balanced. I was not balanced but we both continued to strive to find that utopic state.

My family was one circle, my friends another. I also had work colleagues with whom I maintained contact, neighbors, friends, or just acquaintances that I met at the gym, on my walk, or participating in a volunteer activity.

My goal was to make three people smile every day. But I needed to limit my time on this activity. It could easily have consumed my entire day.

Sandra tried to connect but her circle of friends became smaller and smaller until only Christine and I remained.

I learned to be efficient and plan. This could have been my number one balance activity, but if my mind and body weren't into an activity, it wouldn't get done. I had a planner. My husband used his phone, but I still liked paper and pen. I used my phone to make notes that I transferred to my planner when I returned home. Sandra made lists and loved to strike out what she had accomplished.

I had to learn a lot about funerals and responsibilities when Sandra started her rapid decline. After several months of grieving, I did a podcast for Family Council members across the province about 'End of Life Planning.' It is too easy to be taken advantage of when one is mourning. I advised those who listened to the podcast to take just one item each day, research it, document it, and file it. To tackle this whole project all at once would be depressing. I cautioned my fellow council members not to become overwhelmed and to make sure that they took care of themselves throughout the process. I advised them to chunk their responsibilities down. Make a few phone calls each day. Start by putting a label on a file folder.

When Sandra was living, her name appeared in my planner daily. It was either check with Bendale, check with the government, check with doctors, pick up new socks, or visit.

With a lifetime of bumps in the road, I learned early to expect the unexpected. With five adult children and six grandchildren, there was always something happening that was beyond our control. I would stop, assess, do what I could, and move on. Illness and age were my greatest barriers, stamina and determination my greatest strengths. I often felt that I could do more than my body allowed. I would continue to try, hurt myself, rest, and finally modify my activity.

There were times when achieving balance seemed impossible. The most popular yoga position for balance is called the tree. We were taught to stand with our feet together and our hands at our heart in a prayer position. Then we were instructed to try and lift one foot and place it on the inside of the opposite leg, above or below our knee, but never on our knee. Finally, we slowly raised our hands to the sky and opened our arms.

If I had anything on my mind, if my thoughts wandered, or if my mind was not focused on what I was doing, I could not hold that position. I was not balanced. I learned that by putting my hand on the wall or a nearby chair I could get the feeling of being balanced.

I had an appointment with a medical specialist on July 23, 2019, the day that Sandra died. I saw my doctor, drove to Toronto, and sat by Sandra's side with my sister Christine and her daughter Candy until Sandra passed later that evening.

I would not have been able to hold any position that day, but I always knew that if I was able to breathe, I could do yoga. I could go back to the beginning and the calm would come faster.

Chapter Eleven

LOOK AWAY FROM THE SUN (YEARS 73-77) 2018-2022

If you stare at the sun too long, you will go blind and see nothing. If you look at the side of the sun and take in the surrounding area, you may come away with a whole new perspective. Daniel Bor quoted several newspaper articles and on February 16, 1006 (page 11) he said that if one wants to make a complicated decision, they must stop thinking about it. In the same year, BBC newscasters told decision-makers to 'sleep on it' if they couldn't find the answer. The unconscious mind is your best decision-maker.

I had spent half of my life looking for a sense of balance that would magically transform Sandra and any other family members or descendants who may suffer from problems with living into happy members of society.

I was lost in the trees and could no longer see the forest. Then on June 12, 2018, I was forced to change my focus. My body broke down.

We had returned from Florida in early April. I was feeling okay, but I had several small health concerns. I didn't feel that any one of them was life-threatening, but together they made me feel unwell. Every time I blew my nose, bloody mucous came out of the right nostril. My right ear was sore, and my right sinus area was sore to the touch but nothing that was excruciating or intolerable. I was tired and my hair was breaking and falling out. I had suffered with a thyroid problem for forty years and thought that I might need a medication adjustment. We had moved into our open up our northern residence routine and with the gardening and cleaning, I developed a pain in my right side. I shared my discomfort with Barry and said that I thought I should see a doctor. There was a hospital near our northern home, but I also knew that they weren't equipped to deal with an appendicitis attack or any major surgeries that might be required. I asked Barry to take me home to Waterloo where I could see our family doctor.

The earliest appointment that I could get with our family doctor was June 12th. I had a manicure (French), a pedicure (blue nail polish), and my hair trimmed and styled before I went to see the doctor. My neighbor met me in the driveway and commented on how great I looked and asked where I was going. I told her that I was going to see the doctor and we both laughed.

Once there, our doctor went through the routine checks before asking if I had any concerns. I mentioned that I had this pain in my lower right side. She poked and prodded and then asked if Barry was in the parking lot.

I said, "No."

She asked me to drive home, not eat lunch, and have Barry drive me to the emergency department of one of the local hospitals. She would send over a requisition for an ultrasound.

I drove home and told Barry what the doctor had said. He looked at me and said, "Do I have to? Parking is terrible at the hospital as well as expensive."

On the way to the hospital, he asked what our family doctor thought it was. I said that I didn't know, but the ultrasound was to look at my gall bladder as well as a possible twisted bowel or appendicitis.

We went into the emergency department. I had blood work taken and was asked to sit on a stretcher until someone from ultrasound was able to collect me.

In the meantime, the nurse practitioner in charge came in to see me and asked why I was there. I said that I had this pain in my side.

She looked at me as if to say, "Do you know how busy we are down here?"

When she left, I said that we should not have come.

I went for my ultrasound and then returned to the curtained cubicle. Again the 'why are you here?' nurse came in to tell me that all three ultrasounds were normal.

I asked Barry if he thought we should leave. The nurse practitioner said I had to wait for the blood work to come back. She came back a brief time later and her whole demeanor had changed. She asked me to move to a bed at the end of the row and wait for the on-call doctor to see me. We kept asking how long I would be in the emergency department and when she thought we could go home.

In a kind voice she said, "I shouldn't be the one to tell you this, but I don't think you should plan on going home tonight." Barry and I looked at one another and waited for the doctor.

When he came in, he said that they wanted to monitor me for the evening and would keep me in the emergency department overnight. My ultrasounds were all normal. They had prearranged for a surgeon to standby to remove my gall bladder, but the ultrasound of my gall bladder was normal. We looked at him for more of an explanation. He then shared that my liver enzymes were elevated, and they didn't know why. A normal bilirubin reading was under twenty, mine was 1400.

I felt okay. I thought that I looked good, but four hours later I was up on the seventh floor. There were two other patients in the room divided by curtains. The woman in the bed across from me was dying. The one beside her was waiting for a space to open in a palliative care facility. I don't know if I was told or imagined it, but I kept telling everyone that I was going home tomorrow. Nurses came in regularly to check my vitals and make sure that I was lucid. They started me on Prednisone 40 mg and an IV drip that was designed to encourage blood clotting.

On the night of June 12th, 2018, I saw three doctors within the span of four hours. The first doctor was the doctor on call in the emergency department. The second was a young internist, and the third was taking over from the doctor in the emergency department. He tried to answer as many questions as he could. As he was leaving, he asked if I had any more questions.

I said, "Just one. Can you fix it?"

I was not upset when admitted to hospital. I was tired and needed a rest. Barry went home and returned with a duffel bag filled with clothes and toiletry items. I never did wear a hospital gown. The washroom was like my private washroom because my other two roommates could not get out of bed. A hospital administrator came in and said that I had private coverage, and she could move me to a private room. I said I was going home, and it would be a waste of time. It was the hospital religious counsellor who annoyed me the most. He kept returning and asking if I wanted to talk. I said no and reassured him that I was going home shortly. We were just waiting for my test results to fall into range.

Beginning with this hospital admission, every doctor I met asked me how much alcohol I drank. I kept repeating over and over that I was not a drinker.

The most I ever drank was a 4 ounce glass of wine to participate socially. It was a relief to have an excuse not to drink. I never liked it. I kept saying that alcohol made me tired, and I missed the conversation and company of others. Over the years I added anaesthesia to the alcohol as a substance that I felt that my body could not tolerate. When I had dental work done, I would be in a daze for several days before the anaesthetic totally left my system. It got so bad that I started to have dental work done without freezing.

In my seventies, I compared this phenomenon with Indigenous and Asian peoples who did not seem to be born with an enzyme that would break down alcohol. To my surprise, one dentist had a name for what I was describing (Alcohol dehydrogenase, ADH) and said that some women also lack this enzyme. This was another example of when I listened to my body. I didn't know what I was experiencing, but I knew how my body reacted. Over the years the scientific community confirmed what my body was telling me.

I had experienced weird health issues throughout my life but had only been hospitalized at age 6 for eye surgery and for the natural birth of three children. Barry came with two boys which expanded our family from three to five children. When asked about the last time I was hospitalized, I calmly responded about fifty years ago when my youngest daughter was born. However, every couple of years I saw specialists for concerns that no one could explain.

While I was in the hospital, I washed and dressed every morning, did my hair, and put-on make-up. Barry would come with Tim Horton's coffee and the morning paper, and we would discuss what was happening both in the world and in our little family. Our children were horrified that I had been hospitalized. Barry was too. I was not a sickly person. I was always strong and active. Here I was, hooked up to an intravenous pole that I had to drag to the washroom and everywhere I went. I am a flamboyant dresser and the woman who was waiting for a space in a palliative care facility loved to see me exit the washroom every morning dressed to the nines and ready to go. If she asked me once, she asked me twenty-five times if I was sure that I was going home. I always said yes.

Our children brought me books, treats, and a portable video player with videos to pass the time. A good friend who lived across the street from the hospital brought me fresh fruit and homemade muffins regularly. When hospital staff asked why I did not finish my breakfast, I pointed to my stash, and they smiled. I became a crossword puzzle whiz and tidied and cleaned the areas around my roommates' beds as well as my own.

The nurses recorded my vital statistics every few hours, and after a few days, the intravenous needle was removed. I had developed a routine of dragging the pole with me rather than call for assistance whenever I needed to use the washroom. The first night it was removed, I went through the entire routine and found myself in the washroom with the pole which was attached to nothing!

Barry was there day and night until they would tell him that he had to leave. One visit he even brought Bracken, our beautiful one hundred–pound Doberman, to visit. Bracken was so excited to see me, and I was equally excited to see him. It was a wonderful visit and, of course, the staff smiled as he basked in all the attention.

Father's Day fell within the period of my hospitalization. I told Barry to go to Toronto and have dinner with two of our sons (his boys). He refused. I could not go out to even get him a card. It was time for creative thinking on both of our parts. I found a recipe for sticky buns in one of the magazines I was reading. Barry and I loved stopping at St. Cinnamon's in the mall and sharing one of their buns with a coffee. I gently removed the page from the magazine and wrote on it that when I was home, I would make these for him as his Father's Day gift.

I did make them several weeks later. It took me five hours! The dough needed to rise. I was hoping that he wouldn't like them, but they were delicious. Now we make them together.

Barry topped me and walked in at suppertime with a home-cooked steak dinner. You could smell it all through the hall, and many of the employees looked in, sniffed, and smiled.

Despite all the good things that happened, I was still ill. There was something wrong. The whites of my eyes were yellow, and my blood enzymes were coming down but were still elevated.

I think everyone assumed that I was going to die. I looked around when I woke up every morning to make sure that I was still alive.

My one friend told me that she would write my eulogy. My sister-in-law said that she was waiting for the results of the autopsy. She meant biopsy but said autopsy. Barry started looking for plots and talking cemetery stones.

I just took it all in and decided that if I had anything to do with my body and my health, I would improve. I was not ready to die. Throughout my life I heard my dad's voice say, "Fight, fight, fight the illness" whenever I had one of my weird health episodes.

The woman directly across from my bed was ready to die. Her sons and grandchildren came to visit constantly. The funeral director was also at her side daily. She was there so much that I assumed that she was a family member. My roommate was in pain. One evening I mentally told her that she could go. Her family had all seen her and that they would be all right. She did die that evening, and I was happy that she was no longer in pain but a little spooked that she left after I mentally gave her permission.

A space miraculously came available at the palliative care facility, and my second roommate was gone the next day also. Before she left, we wished each other well and she told me how much she enjoyed seeing me all dressed up and ready to go home. She asked if I still thought I was going home and I said, "Absolutely."

It would be another two days before I left and during that time, I shared the room with two elderly gentlemen. One was totally bedridden, and the other was waiting for dialysis. He was confused. He told his wife that he liked sharing a room with a beautiful woman. His wife told him to behave himself and I laughed.

Two orderlies had to help him from his wheelchair into his bed. When his wife left, he wanted to use the washroom. He pressed the buzzer and a young PSW came in and asked if he could undress by himself.

He said, "Yes."

I said, "No."

Then she asked if he could go to the bathroom by himself if she gave him a walker.

He said, "Yes."

I said, "No."

I shared the interaction with his wife when she returned. She thanked me several times. She spoke with the staff about his confusion and his limitations. Two orderlies helped him undress and use the washroom.

By this time, I was getting bored. I was no longer attached to an I.V., and I asked if I could walk the floor. They said yes and I began my several circles a day. I added yoga exercises on the bed and insisted on taking a shower. There were no showers for patients on this floor, so I used the staff showers.

I was discharged with the diagnosis of Autoimmune Hepatitis and given instructions to return for a liver biopsy, a requisition for blood work, and an appointment with a local internist.

Because I was admitted directly from the emergency department when I arrived at my designated time for the biopsy, they had no record that I had ever been a patient in the hospital. The biopsy was normal. The ultrasound was normal. The blood work was improving.

I met with the internist a few weeks later in mid-July. He made an appointment for me to see a liver specialist in late August.

When I met with Dr. Paul Marotta, the liver specialist, he reviewed my tests and asked why I was referred to him. I reviewed my past two months of care and investigation. He did a fibrin test which measured the amount of scarring in my liver. He then asked how much I alcohol I drank. I said that I was almost an abstainer, but he would continue to ask me that same question for the following six months. My fibrin test recorded thirty-nine out of forty. I asked what that meant, and he said that I had stage four cirrhosis of the liver. At a measurement of forty my liver would shut down and I would die. He was very blunt, but I liked that. He did, however, reduce the amount of medication that I was taking based on my blood work. I started a 'good-bye drawer' where I kept a file folder outlining music and pictures that I would like at my funeral.

By the end of September, my enzyme numbers had improved to the point that I was only on 5 mg of Prednisone (down from 40 mg in the hospital) and I felt surprisingly good. I was back at the gym taking classes about three times a week. The husband of one of my instructors was experiencing a similar challenge with his liver at exactly the same time.

I had blood work every two weeks. I tired easily, so Barry and I reduced our activities. We continued to go to the movies, theater, craft shows, visit tourist spots within driving distance, visit our children, and be "Uber" drivers for our granddaughters, driving them to and from gymnastics.

My next appointment with the liver specialist was December 28th. I had an ultrasound booked for December and an appointment with the local internist. I had a team of three doctors: our family doctor, a local internist, and a visiting liver specialist.

It was late October when I received a call from our family doctor's office saying that the flu shots were available for vulnerable and elderly patients. Even in my mid-seventies, I never thought of myself as elderly. I asked if they thought I should have the flu shot given my compromised immune system and the fact that I always had problems with flu shots. I only started getting flu shots because Sandra was in a long-term care facility, and I did not want to take any viruses in. Now, I wanted the flu shot to also protect me from catching anything when I visited her.

Our family doctor said, "Absolutely get the flu shot. We are expecting a bad flu this year and you need all the protection that you can get. The flu shot is not a 'live virus.' You can't get the flu from the shot."

I had been told the same thing for years, but I would become terribly ill after I received it. A lab technician in Toronto advised me to get the shot in two doses like a baby to minimize any side effects. I convinced our family doctor to agree to the two doses, but from the look on her face, I knew that she didn't believe a word of what I said. I was the only adult patient in her whole practice who received the flu shot in half doses.

I then called my local internist to ask his opinion. He said the same thing. The flu shot would not affect my liver, and it was necessary that I get it before the start of flu season.

My gym instructor's husband who was struggling with liver issues caught a virus and died.

I had heard from two of my team of doctors that it was impossible for the flu shot to affect my liver enzyme numbers, but I was not convinced. I called the liver specialist. He said that I would die from pneumonia or a heart attack before my liver failed. He advised me to get the flu shot.

I got my first half flu shot on the 9th of November 2018. My bilirubin went from under 20 (normal) to five hundred overnight. The specialist called while we were at the One-of-a-Kind craft show in Toronto and increased my medication.

Three weeks later, I repeated the whole round of questioning before I booked an appointment for the second half of my flu shot. All three doctors said that the increase in my bilirubin numbers could not have been a result of the flu shot.

I had the second half of my flu shot in early December. My bilirubin numbers went from 500 to 900 overnight.

The specialist called from London and increased my Prednisone again. Barry and I were in Niagara-on-the-Lake to see the play "A Christmas Carol" at the Shaw Festival.

My local internist said that he was stepping down from my team. My ultrasound was within normal range, and he did not feel qualified to deal with what I was experiencing. He did not feel that he had anything to add. I thanked him for his honesty. A year later our family doctor apologized for not listening to me about the flu shot.

By mid-December 2018, I wondered whether I would ruin Christmas by dying before year end.

On December 28th, 2018, Dr. Marotta arranged for a second fibrin test.

I said, "I'm not going to get better, am I?"

He said, "No."

The technician administered the test measuring the amount of scarring. She looked at Dr. Marotta. He asked for the wand and redid the test himself. The result was thirty-eight out of forty. I had improved.

I spent all of 2019 fighting what we thought were the results of the flu shot and the added complications of being on Prednisone for such an extended period of time.

I read. I researched. I put together ideas to explain what I was experiencing. At this time, I figured that I could have something that was hereditary and if I did nothing else, I wanted to leave this world with someone smarter than me investigating that possibility and assisting my descendants and hopefully others.

I met with the liver specialist every three months and continued to search for reasons beyond those that had been presented to me. At the end of my March meeting with Dr. Marotta, I slid across one of my ideas. I did the same thing I had done when I was searching for a balanced life for Sandra. I examined my life in detail, only this time I focused on medical problems and idiosyncrasies that kept occurring throughout my life. I documented all my experiences that I felt might be relevant to my body reacting in strange ways by exhibiting symptoms that were never fully explained.

My lifelong documentation exercise proved fruitless in my search to help Sandra. I could not transfer my balanced lifestyle to Sandra. It seemed like a dead end.

There was still something that bonded Sandra and me. I could still communicate with her. I continued to search for that link. Time and time again when Sandra experienced psychotic episodes, she would tell me that it was okay. It was just allergies. Every spring and every fall, our family prepared ourselves for extreme behavior. We made every excuse under the sun, from Sandra being an alcoholic, to her frying her brain with drugs when she was young, to her not being able to manage the memories of family members dying. Sandra was on thyroid medication and continually told us that she had been diagnosed with Hepatitis C many years previously. No one listened.

None of the thoughts in the previous paragraph were front and center when I was faced with a physical illness of my own. My only thought was that I had to get better. I was of no use to anyone if I could not function. Barry drove us to our northern home for me to recuperate. I was worried that we were a four-hour drive from our medical support system, but in the end, it turned out to be the best possible decision.

I was not in any pain, only weak and extremely tired. Prednisone was supposed to cause me to gain weight and suffer from insomnia. It did the opposite. I had to struggle to maintain my weight and it caused me to sleep. I kept asking what symptoms I should be looking for that would indicate when something was wrong. I was told it would be yellowing of the eyes, abdominal pain, black stools indicating internal bleeding, and/or mental confusion. If I ever became disoriented and confused, I was to go to the nearest emergency department.

Dr. Marotta added 4 Myfortic a day. Myfortic is a 'transplant' support drug. It confused me because I had been told that I was not a candidate for a transplant, that I was too old at 73 years of age, and that my body would not survive the surgery. I never did ask why I was being given a transplant support drug. I just knew that I was on a lot of medication, and I was unable to write. When I tried to write in the early days of my illness, I would review my work the following day in shock at all the errors I had made. I would describe my mental state as having a 'foggy brain.' Barry tried to do everything— cook, clean, and take care of me. Rather than be grateful, I was annoyed. It felt as if he was trying to control my life. I hated it and became difficult and hurtful with my comments. I needed to get better. I put Sandra and my search for indicators that might assist in improving her life aside to focus on my own issues. However, I always managed her finances and any administrative issues that arose.

Chapter Twelve

MY MEDICAL HISTORY
(YEARS 3 MONTHS-75) 1945-2020

I returned to my initial strategy of looking at anything and everything that had happened in my own life to see if there might be a clue to my present situation.

There is much progress being made in medicine. However, with that progress comes the loss of individuality. We are not machines. We are not transformers.

Blood tests, ultrasounds and X-Rays do not tell the entire story, and just as I documented past experiences to search for a reason for Sandra's struggles, I began documenting my medical experiences to look for any recurring problems or patterns. Earlier chapters document the investigation of the mind, while this chapter documents the investigation of my physical body. I had always lived a life that proposed the benefits of a mind/body connection, but somehow the actual physical body always got the short end of the stick.

When we moved from Toronto to Waterloo, I asked our new family doctor if she wanted me to contact our family doctor in Toronto so she could forward my files and my medical history for her to review. To my surprise, she said no. She said that we would deal with any issues as they arose. I told her that I had experienced some very weird illnesses throughout my life. They just came and went, and, to date, no one had been able to identify the cause. It would be ten years before the next serious medical issue arose, and two years after that before my hospitalization with a diagnosis of autoimmune hepatitis.

I believed that the rationale behind my being diagnosed as having autoimmune hepatitis had something to do with my 40-year struggle with my thyroid. As mentioned previously, part of my thyroid had been destroyed with a radioactive iodine capsule. I was told that the portion of the thyroid that remained should have been enough to function, but for whatever reason it did not. It was pointed out that it might 'kick-in' at some time in the future and I should be monitored regularly. After 40 years of monitoring and minor medication changes, I continued to take Synthroid daily.

The thyroid is the body's regulator. "It is a small, butterfly-shaped gland, measuring about two inches that lies just under the skin below the Adam's apple in the neck. It's a part of the endocrine system, which is made up of glands that produce, store, and release hormones. Hormones produced by the thyroid gland, triiodothyronine (T3) and thyroxine (T4) have an enormous impact on your health, affecting all aspects of your metabolism.[3]"

Thyroid malfunction or disease is hereditary and tends to surface in women between 20 and 30 years of age.

I hoped my search would help with recovery and an understanding of what I was now facing. When I was still living with my mom, she had shared that at 3 months of age, I had contracted both measles and chickenpox at the same time. My parents were prepared for me to die. My two older brothers had documented cases of each separate illness. There was no way of confirming whether this, in fact, was true since both parents and brothers were deceased.

I was told that my parents took me to the doctor as an infant because I used to crawl into the basement and eat coal. The doctor said that I was lacking something that I found in the coal and not to worry. In my search for answers, I read an article on nutrition that states an individual's lack of thiamine can lead to chronic deficiencies of B1. Plants, bacteria, and fungi all manufacture their own thiamine, but animals are incapable of making this vitamin and must get it from food. Synthetic forms have made their way into our food and vitamins.[4] Synthetic thiamine is not found in nature but created from coal tar derivatives among other toxic substances. I wondered if this was something I was looking for in the coal bin.

In elementary school, I was very petite, and, out of five siblings, I was the only one given free milk. My mother had also been given free milk at school. I never reached my full five-foot seven inch height until I was in high school.

At age 13/14, my parents called the doctor to the house because I was severely ill. The doctor asked if a snake could have bitten me. We lived in downtown Toronto. I was treated with antibiotics and rest. At age 15 or 16, I was diagnosed with rheumatic fever and told that I would have a heart murmur for the rest of my life. Again, the doctor treated me with antibiotics and added a year of rest. I relayed this story to every doctor I have seen since then. Despite what the doctor said about a heart murmur after having rheumatic fever, no other doctor has ever heard the murmur.

At ages 21, 22 and 27, I delivered three healthy babies. With my first pregnancy (at Women's College Hospital), I experienced a severe urinary tract infection (UTI) which was treated with a sulphur antibiotic.

I was followed in their UTI clinic for the last four months of my pregnancy. When I arrived at the hospital to deliver, they had no record of me being followed by an obstetrician. I explained the UTI clinic but was not prepared for the gas that I was given to ease my delivery. I kept shouting, "No." The attending medical staff ignored my words. I vomited at the same time as I was delivering. The staff were disgusted, and I was embarrassed.

I had an IUD inserted to allow for a future planned pregnancy . Fourteen months later I was posing for pictures for a medical article on the failure of IUDs. The device came out with the delivery of our beautiful baby boy. My body did not seem to accept foreign implants, and as much as I didn't like Dr. Marotta's comment that I was 'too old' for a transplant, I rationalized that my body would probably not have accepted it anyway.

At age 31, when I first showed signs of thyroid trouble, doctors kept an eye on my case. Then in 2016, the thyroid symptoms took a turn. The smallest change in dosage alleviated adverse symptoms.

While we lived in Toronto, I experienced many health issues that could never be explained. Our family doctor, Dr. Lorraine Philp, referred me to numerous specialists over the years to try and solve my unusual health challenges.

Each time I had an episode, I described what I felt was a 'growth, a cyst, a tumour,' something that held some sort of fluid. This sac of fluid put pressure on my left upper back and sometimes my left breast area. It could be so severe at times that it caused me to walk crooked. I may or may not experience lower right-sided pain, depending on the season or foods that I had eaten. For many years we blamed shrimp and wine at Christmas. I have since learned that I should have been describing the 'sac of fluid' as an 'abscess' which was beyond my limited knowledge at the time.

My first referral was to an internist. He took my SED rate (Sedation rate measures the amount of inflammation in the body). It was many years ago, but I remember him saying that a normal SED rate was between zero and twenty; mine was seventy. The revised normal range for women is 0 to 29. He didn't know how I got up in the morning or how I walked into his office and was standing there before him. Again, I was treated with antibiotics, but an anti-inflammatory was added.

In the late 1990s, I experienced an angry red left breast. We thought that our 80 pound Doberman had jumped up and accidentally scratched me. The area of the scratch expanded, and the breast continued to turn a dark red. It was warm to the touch but not painful. I was referred to a breast surgeon who wished me good luck and referred me to Princess Margaret Hospital. Several doctors and many interns came into the room where I lay on a stretcher with a towel covering the affected breast. The oncologist lifted the covering, and six interns examined my breast. I was immediately sent for an ultrasound which showed nothing. You might guess how they treated that problem: antibiotics and anti-inflammatories.

I saw an allergist who said that I was allergic to cats and a rheumatologist who found nothing serious but 'crooked fingers.' She diagnosed me as suffering from osteoarthritis.

My next challenge was breathing. I need to point out here that I never went into the doctor's office complaining of most of these illnesses. Anomalies showed up on blood tests after each annual physical. The main complaint I had was about the periodic 'abscesses' that appeared here and there on the inside of my body. There was never anything, other than the red breast, to see externally. What I am calling internal abscesses were extremely painful, but by the time I had an ultrasound, they had disappeared or they may not have even showed up on an ultrasound at that time.

My oxygen level was below normal on a routine annual physical. My doctor referred me to a respirologist. He said that I had 'severe asthma.' I asked what the other descriptors were, and he said, 'mild to moderate.' He gave me a puffer and followed my progress for the next eight years. I had never had asthma as a child. He questioned my environment, and I told him that my husband had built us a new house. He told me that it was the new house that was causing my challenges and that they would lessen over time.

Somewhere along the way, I saw a cardiologist who diagnosed me as suffering from costochondritis. It may have been one of these weird abscesses that were painful. This time the pain was in my chest. He treated me with antibiotics and rest.

Shortly afterward, Dr. Tony Graham (St. Michael's Hospital) started me on Lipitor 20 mg as a form of prevention.

Both my brothers had died from cardiomyopathy (enlarged hearts) at ages 55 and 60. No one knew that heart disease was a factor in our family history, but both brothers were heavy smokers and moderate drinkers, so we attributed their early deaths to poor lifestyles.

Dr. Graham was Chairman of the Board at the Heart and Stroke Foundation when I was Vice-President of Regional Services. I trusted his judgement. I saw Dr. Graham for several years, but because I worked out regularly at a gym and in a pool and taught yoga, they had a hard time getting my heart rate elevated. The staff soon asked why I was coming and my yearly assessments at St. Michael's Hospital came to a halt.

In August 2009, I had taken Barry to Great Bear Lake for a fishing trip at Plummer's Lodge. It was his 60th birthday present. Part of his gift was that I would go with him. I was not really a 'fisher person' so I listened closely to whatever the guide said. I was the only woman in the lodge, and much to the dismay of the male expert anglers, I caught the largest fish of the week, a 42-pound trout. According to the tournament rules, no one was allowed to help me bring my catch in, and I did struggle, but I did eventually land my trophy. In hindsight it should not have been a surprise to anyone. Even though everyone paid their individual guides a lot of money for advice and direction to excellent fishing spots, the men, being men, would argue with their guide and say that they had their favorite lures that would land them the prize fish! I, on the other hand, just became an extension of our guide. I listened to his every word, followed his every instruction, and used whatever lure he recommended. Flying home from Yellowknife, I developed shingles in my upper left back.

I could never seem to be in total control of my physical health. Just as Sandra struggled with her mental balance, my physical balance was a challenge throughout my life.

I would have bouts of pneumonia each winter. They were treated with antibiotics and rest. Barry and I both got pneumonia shots to try and avoid future episodes. Once I retired and we started wintering in Florida, my winter illnesses seemed to subside for several years. I felt physically balanced but will never know whether it was the sun, the additional activity, or the reduced stress after I retired. I did, however, become the first Canadian and first female President of the Pelican Lake Motor Coach Park, so there was always some stress. I also continued to chair the Bendale Acres Family Council and ran the monthly meetings by conference call.

In April 2017, Barry and I went to St. Lucia with our eldest son, his wife, and our twin granddaughters. I developed a hacking cough. Local workers said it was likely from the volcanic ash and that it affected some people the way it had affected me. I also developed a cold sore on my face, something I hadn't experienced in over 20 years. Barry had flu-like symptoms for a day, but my severe cough persisted even after our return home. Our son and his family experienced nothing. Once again, I was treated with antibiotics and rest.

In August 2017, when we were at our northern home, I experienced a pain in my upper left arm area but no cough or fever. I went to the emergency department of the Barry's Bay Hospital where medical staff conducted routine blood tests and took a chest X-Ray. The doctor on call said that my blood tests were normal, similar to 2009 when I went in for painkillers for shingles. I shrugged, said okay, and started to dress. The doctor came in again and apologized. She hadn't seen my chest X-Ray when she first spoke with me. I had pneumonia. I was treated with antibiotics. I didn't feel that I needed any rest.

In February/March 2018, Barry and I rented a house in Naples, Florida. We felt our coaching years were coming to an end, so we sold our lot in Florida and eventually sold our coach. The beaches in Naples were closed to the public due to something called Red Tide. It was a red algae bloom that floated on top of the water and was killing fish and large water life (dolphins, sharks, manatees) up and down the coast. The fear was that it may become airborne. In addition, there was a lot of smoke from fires along 'Alligator Alley.' We also complained about black mold in the private pool area that was attached to the house we had rented.

I would wake up throughout the month of March with blood in my nose. It was more prevalent on my right side. This bloody mucous continued for many months. I also experienced a thickness on the inside of my throat, more on the left side than the right. I think that I was able to control the thickness with diet (less dairy) but that may all be in my head. I did notice small, sore-like pimples on my scalp whenever I washed my hair.

All of this led up to my admission to the hospital on June 12, 2018. No one cared about my past medical history, but like Sandra before me, I always felt that there was something missing with the current diagnosis and treatment that I was receiving. Where was the balance in my own life that I struggled and failed to find for my sister?

Chapter Thirteen
A POPULATION OF ONE
(YEARS 73-77) 2018-2022

After Sandra died on July 23, 2019, I had already come to terms with the fact that just finding or teaching her balance skills would not cure her. There was something else lurking in our background that caused me to look at the world much differently.

After my autoimmune hepatitis diagnosis, I was thinking that my time on this earth was limited, and I needed to take responsibility for tracking my own path of improvement.

In August 2018, my fibrin test (the measurement of scarring on my liver) was thirty-nine out of forty. I was in stage 4 cirrhosis of the liver. In December 2018, when I asked if the scarring could improve, the doctor said, "No."

The test was done, and the number was thirty-eight out of forty. It was repeated and yielded the same results. Six months later the reading showed up at 37-38, and in December 2019, the numbers were 36 to 37. In September 2020, the numbers dropped to 34 to 35. I was still in stage four but there definitely was improvement. On January 7th, 2021, Barry watched the monitor. He stood up. I sat up and we both asked at the same time, "Did you say 24?"

Dr. Marotta confirmed the number but pointed out that 'normal' was below 15. We were happy with the direction.

It had been a long two-and-a-half years and the side effects from the prednisone were horrible. I couldn't write; the medication left me with a foggy brain. I had large black hairs grow out of the corners of my eyes that had to be plucked. I felt like wolfman. I developed somewhat of a 'moon face' that was puffy and swollen. My sunken eyes made me look like a tired zombie. My long, beautiful hair became thin and broke easily. The medication that was recommended to protect my bones made me dizzy and I was forced to stop. The calcium supplement would have caused me to fall before a broken bone would.

Then in September 2019, I developed diabetes from the extended time that I had been on prednisone. Dr. Briones was added to my medical team—the endocrinologist who had treated my thyroid problem for many years. I never knew that she dealt with diabetes as well. She knew immediately that my diabetes was prednisone-induced, and she added the drug Metformin to be taken twice a day. I bruised easily, developed red spots on my arms, and my feet swelled to the point that made walking difficult. My blood pressure increased because of the prednisone. Another medication to control my blood pressure was added. I became a walking pharmacy.

For someone who had only taken two prescribed medications for 40 years with no aches, no pains, and no headaches, this was a massive change. The pharmacy kept asking if they could monitor my medication schedule. I adamantly said, "No."

My medication changed so frequently that when I was asked how I felt, I started to answer, "I think I feel fine. What does my blood work say?"

All my ultrasounds were normal.

I started looking for triggers, something that might have set off my immune system to fight the trigger and then have it turn and start attacking healthy tissue (my liver). I documented food products, plants and flowers, building products, and any other allergens I thought of. If Barry asked me once, he asked me a hundred times to stop playing doctor. I kept reading and researching.

We got a phone call from an acquaintance in Florida who was following in our travel footsteps. She felt that she and her husband were getting too old to "bus" (drive a motor coach) to Florida and stay in a coach park. They knew that we had sold our bus and the last year we were in Florida, we rented a house in a gated community. They wanted to know what the rules were with regards to dogs in the housing complex. She asked how I was, and Barry said that I had been diagnosed with autoimmune hepatitis.

She said, "Oh, I've had that for 25 years!" Barry and I looked at each other and wondered why no one had told us that you could live with this disease for many years. She was on one drug, but every so often prednisone had to be pre-scribed for short periods of time to bring her body back into a balanced state.

On our next scheduled visit with Dr. Marotta, the liver specialist, I relayed the comments of our friend in Florida. I said that I didn't know that you could live a long time with autoimmune hepatitis. He said he didn't know either. Ap-parently, no one was studying that particular illness. There were few cases in Canada, and it was only when he dug into the research because of my situation that he learned that some individuals live a long time with the disease and that some children are even born with it.

My mind went back to a conversation that I had had with a former col-league whose husband had been diagnosed with the same illness less than ten years prior. At that time, she told me that her husband Don had an extremely rare autoimmune disease and there were less than ten documented cases in the world. Don lived about eight years after being diagnosed. She felt that if they had known that he should have had an ultrasound every six months, he might still be alive today.

Barry and I continued to document the timing of my ultrasounds, which were all normal. We took responsibility to prompt our family doctor to book the screening.

I was encouraged. I knew from the years that I worked in a doctor's office that doctors didn't know everything. I wasn't being judgemental. There are as many anomalies in the world as there are people. I read Dr. Lisa Saunders' book *Every Patient Tells a Story* in which doctors describe their most difficult diagnoses, mistakes and all.

Dr. Saunders comments (page 106) that, "It's a truism in medicine that dif-ficult diagnoses are most likely to be made by the most or least experienced doc-tors. . .The most senior have a broad set of experiences that allows them to consider many different possibilities. Because they are open to a wide variety of observations, fewer pertinent findings are filtered out. What about the novice? They have no expectations and there is some evidence that this lack of pre-set experience-based biases allows them to look more carefully at the entire picture."

What did I learn from this brief exploration into my disease?

Patients need to take responsibility for their own health.

Barry and I had to be vigilant in keeping track of doctor appointments, blood work, medications, and screenings. We were working with three doctors, and they were all busy. None had my file constantly in front of them. I remember arguing with more than one of my doctors saying I wanted to know what 'caused' this illness. What was the trigger that I could remove? How could I prevent this from happening again? The response was that if doctors knew that they would just have to remove the trigger and I would not have to take medication. It made sense to me, but no one was willing to assist me in my search. They would treat the symptom as it appeared in my bloodwork, but no one had time to investigate the cause.

I could have many years of life ahead of me.

If I were careful, I would not necessarily leave this earth soon. This realization evolved over a few years. It would have removed so much angst if one of the doctors had shared the parameters of my illness earlier. Perhaps they didn't know.

When my bilirubin numbers spiked after each half of a flu shot, I asked the internist if I would ruin Christmas (December 2018). He just said that he had several patients who had lived for several years. I asked how many years. He said eight but qualified that statement by saying that he had only been practicing and seeing patients for eight years.

Our next key learning was more of a surprise than learning. No individual researcher, or no research team, seemed to be studying this disease. If anyone was going to add any information to this big black hole, it had to be me.

Learning that some children are born with autoimmune hepatitis inspired me to investigate further.

The Mayo Clinic[5] (as of March 12, 2022) lists the primary symptoms and causes of immunodeficiency. Heredity is still considered the primary cause, but the warning signs and symptoms were of most interest to me.

It took me 75 years to be able to properly articulate what was going on inside my body. Blood levels going up and down would not identify, confirm, or even identify any of the pain or difficulties I experienced.

---

[5] https://www.mayoclinic.org

Chapter Fourteen

THINKING OUTSIDE THE BOX

"The important thing in science is not so much to obtain new facts as to discover new ways of thinking about them."

- (Sir William Bagg)

I look 'normal.' When I cleaned her up, Sandra looked 'normal.' Autistic children look 'normal.' Dr. David Rowland recently (July 2020) published an article in the Journal of Neurology, Psychiatry and Brain Research titled, "Autism as an Intellectual Lens." Dr. Rowland acknowledges that he has an autistic brain. He describes autism as a specialized way of functioning. My mind went back to the television show, "The Good Doctor" and how brilliant the lead character, who lives with autism, functions.

In his examination of the personal lives of historical figures, Rowland proposes that "Thomas Jefferson (1749-1826), Charles Darwin (1809-1882), Thomas Edison (1847-1931), and Albert Einstein (1879-1955) all functioned with autistic hyper focus."

I wondered if it were possible that some of what we currently call mental illnesses are not psychological illness at all. Could the symptoms be the negative side of an evolutionary positive, a physical illness that has not been accurately diagnosed, one that has been incorrectly diagnosed, or a side effect of a prescribed medication used to treat an unrelated illness?

The negative side of an evolutionary positive: What if those who are currently being treated to become 'normal' (whatever that is) are quite naturally exploring parts of their brains that many of us are unable to access without stimulation. Theory used to propose that we only use 10 percent of our brain, leaving 90 percent unused. We now know that is not true. We use our whole brain, but have we ever considered that just as athletes or bodybuilders develop their physical bodies above and beyond the norm, some of us may have the ability to explore and develop human 'creative and survival instincts' above and beyond the norm?

For centuries people have tried to chemically access the part of the brain that allows them to see the future. Carbon dating suggests that First Nations used peyote cacti[6] as early as 3780 BC to foretell the future, even though they experienced 'terrible visions' in the process.[7] It is still allowed today by members of the Native American Church if it is used in the 'spiritual context.'

A whole generation of young people who are (were) not considered mentally ill and who use(d) recreational drugs to explore the deeper recesses of their minds continue to perform in society. Steve Jobs credited "eye opening drugs" with helping "spark the creativity within." Jobs is quoted as saying that "LSD … was a positive life-*changing* experience," and he was glad that he went through that experience.

Some need assistance to explore the deep recesses of their brains, and for whatever evolutionary reason, some may not. Try to imagine how frightening the world must be for a child, young adult, or even an adult who does not take stimulants or enhancers but who 'sees' what others don't.

"Sometimes evolution comes with negative side effects." [8]

"The best example of this is sickle cell anemia. Sickle cell anemia causes red blood cells to take on a curved, crescent-like shape" (Omer Gokcumen) which can lead to severe anemia and death. It occurs in individuals from African heritage. The mutation may occur when individuals move out of their native-born habitat into areas of high altitude. The altitude becomes a trigger to set the mutation in motion.

The positive side of this evolutionary mutation is that those individuals who continue to live in Africa and carry this gene are protected against malaria. This is a huge evolutionary positive. Sickle cell anemia isn't the only example of an evolutionary positive with a negative side effect. One Tay Sachs gene can

---

[6] https://www.verywellmind.com/how-long-does-peyote-stay-in-your-system-80310
[7] peyote.net
[8] Jennifer Viegas, February 3, 2015, *Discovery*

provide protection against tuberculosis and has been linked to high intelligence in Ashkenazi Jews. Having more than one of these genes has been linked to breast cancer.[9]

If researchers studying various brain disorders spent as much time investigating whether there is a positive, creative side to the disorder they are examining, rather than trying to fit everyone into a normal mold, we may not be missing a huge opportunity to see, understand, and explore a possible evolutionary positive.

Many brain disorders are, "Not just about biology or just about environment but an interaction of the two."[10]

I was left with questions about the body (my story). I was left with questions about the mind (Sandra's story).

The first seven chapters of this book deal with my story; what I remember from my childhood, my physical illnesses, and my struggles to maintain a sense of mental and physical balance as I tried to help Sandra find hers. I was left wondering what 'normal' was.

It was like thunderbolt thinking when I realized that I was walking the talk. My whole life had been dedicated to "bringing the body, mind, and spirit into balance and harmony."[11] I kept focusing on the body when I talked about me and the mind when I talked about Sandra. The spirit flowed constantly in and out of both of our lives and that was the bond that kept us communicating.

Everyone yelled at Sandra throughout her adolescence and told her, "Don't take drugs." Many family members argued that by taking drugs, Sandra, "Did it to herself."

Am I being too simplistic in my theory? Possibly, but I can't help noticing how simplistic some of the 'cures' are when society finally recognizes and acknowledges the cause.

In her book *The Bone Garden*, Tess Gerritson[12] writes about women being terrified of childbirth in the 1830s. "They knew that if they went into the hospital to have a baby, there was a good chance that they would come out in a coffin. They were killed by their own doctors. In those days they had no con-

---

[9] Jon Entine, March 2015; genetic literacy project

[10] *The Bipolar Disorder Survival Guide* by David Miklowitz, second edition, 2011, page 11

[11] Christina Brown, *The Book of Yoga*, 2003

[12] *The Bone Garden*, Tess Gerritson, p, 329

cept of germ theory. They wore no gloves, so doctors used their bare hands to examine women. They'd perform an autopsy on a corpse that was putrid with disease, then they'd go to the maternity ward with filthy hands. They'd examine patient after patient, spreading infection right down a row of beds, killing every woman they touched."

Could society be working against us reaching our full potential with humanity moving toward a higher level of consciousness with some of our current treatments like anti-psychotic drugs and electroconvulsive therapy? I have the same question that author Robert Kolker writes about. In *Hidden Valley Road*, he wonders, "What sort of early interventions might have helped them (the brothers documented in the book) before the medications took their toll, neutralizing them without curing them?"[13] (page 334) I always wondered why our brothers died so young (ages 55 and 60) of heart disease when, as far as we knew, there was no heart disease in our family. Jim Galvin, one of the brothers Robert Kolker wrote about, had his death (at age 53) recorded as due to "heart failure, related to his use of neuroleptic drugs. A rare life-threatening disorder most often caused by the drugs meant to help."

Reading this book and these quotes brought tears to my eyes as I thought of how often I encouraged Bob (bipolar) and Sandra (bipolar/schizophrenic tendencies) to listen to the drug recommendations that were meant to stabilize them and allow them to live a normal, balanced life.

---

[13] Robert Kolker, *Hidden Valley Road*, p. 261

Chapter Fifteen

SIMILAR BUT DIFFERENT

Sandra focused on mental balance while paying attention to her physical needs. She wrote in her journal that she: "Didn't do too much of any one drug today. Took one or two smokes with Bob. Took two aspirins, two Tylenol (plain), my three Haldols, and two 50mg Gravols. I guess I should have some cheerios for fibre." (September 10, 1991)

She used drugs and alcohol to quiet her mental demons. She walked miles every day and made sure that she ate what she felt her body needed. She was kind to a fault, giving money to beggars and candy to children. Sandra always kept traditional religion in her thoughts and actions. She had a work ethic but found it hard to maintain employment as she searched for a set of 'rules' to follow to help her gain a sense of balance. Her physical walking and eating what her body craved kept Sandra's heart strong.

Staff told us when she was admitted to the long-term care facility that Sandra may live with her dementia for three years. She died eleven years later.

There was many a time that I prayed for her heart to give out. She did not want to be there. But her heart was strong, and she struggled to survive, always hoping to improve.

I focused on maintaining my physical life balance while always keeping a mental eye on my mind as I struggled to assist Sandra in her search. I walked and added yoga, swimming, and, later, the gym. The addition of new activities extended my circle of friends who continued to lift me up when I needed their support or encouragement. Like all siblings of those suffering from diagnosed mental challenges, there was always a cloud in the background that I feared would burst and cause me to move to the side of struggling with my own mental balance. I remember when my brother Bob died; every cell in my being extolled my pain. There was no sound, only hurt that extended beyond my body. Within twenty-four hours, five friends called from various parts of North America just to touch base and ask how I was feeling. They didn't know that my brother had died but when I reached out with my mind, they 'heard me.'

Documenting our journeys has reinforced how similar we are and how different we are. Seeing the content of my memories and the content of Sandra's memories makes me sad that I could not have done more while she was alive. I kept her physically safe, but in the end, I wonder if she would have chosen a different path. More than once over the years that Sandra was in long term care, I would say, "You don't want to be here, do you?" At first, she just said, "No." Later she would just move her head signifying no, and, finally she just told me with her eyes. If the 'right to choose' her time to leave this world were available when Sandra was lucid and could speak, I know what route she would have chosen.

Having struggled with a 'foggy brain' due to physical illness and medication, I wondered how much her physical condition played a part in Sandra's diagnosis. Was there something in our genes that needed to be identified and harnessed? Could this 'foggy brain' be a negative indicator of an evolutionary positive, a physical malfunction of an evolving body or an iatrogenic result of medication.

Dr. Lynn DeLisi studied schizophrenia because she felt that it was a real neurological disease of the brain and a "study of schizophrenia as a physical ailment" was not in fashion. [14] In 1978, Elliot Gershon felt that the best way to study the genetics of the disease was to study not just the sick people in the family but everyone…. if researchers could somehow find a genetic abnormality that appears in only the sick members of the family and not the well ones, then there would be the genetic smoking gun for schizophrenia." [15]

In the many years of study, there are two avenues that have not been considered. First, are there any positive genetic traits in the family members who are considered well? Lynn DeLisi "was amazed by the good cheer"[16] that Mimi Galvin, matriarch of the Galvin family, displayed throughout her life. The

---

[14] Kolker, page 143
[15] Kolker, p. 146-147
[16] Kolker, page 203

Galvin family included twelve children: ten male and two female. Six boys were diagnosed, medicated, and/or hospitalized with either schizophrenic or bipolar tendencies. Throughout Mimi's life, which included support for a husband who had extramarital affairs and eventually suffered a debilitating stroke, Mimi lived in a dream world. It was her family, and she loved each one of them. Mimi insisted that the disease (gene) came from Don, her husband, because he had been hospitalized for depression earlier in his life.[17] Upon his death, Don's brain was preserved for future scientists to examine and study. In 2016, Lynn DeLisi and one of her cohorts, Stefan McDonogh, published in Molecular Psychiatry that "at least some varieties of mental illness exist on a spectrum" [18] and some mutations come from the mother's side. Remembering that Sandra had a thyroid condition and stated many times that she had been diagnosed with Hepatitis C, I decided to investigate our family's medical history.

Twenty-five years after our mom's death, both Sandra and I continued with our struggles to improve, to find answers to our mental and physical health, and to feel balanced and normal.

I had gone from documenting my life to documenting my physical health history.

I spent several years looking for answers by trying to document and follow my dad's family tree.

Although the search was minimal, nothing really stood out as a possibility or cause. I extended my search.

I started by linking both physical and mental symptoms of family members. Both Christine and I suffered from abscesses over the years. Christine received more attention because her abscesses were external and highly visible. Mine were internal and not visible to any form of examination. Both of us were treated with antibiotics. June, one of our cousins and our mother's niece, was plagued with boils during her younger years and although I never saw any connection, I now wonder if there might be some familial connection between 'boils' and 'abscesses.' Sandra and I were both treated for malfunctioning thyroid conditions. Both Sandra and I had been diagnosed with problems with our liver. Our mom died of colon cancer that had started in her liver and our brother Bob was hospitalized for jaundice the year before he died. Sandra was definitely disoriented and confused throughout most of her life.

---

17 Kolker, page 272
18 Kolker, page 272

Bob exhibited symptoms before he was diagnosed as suffering from bipolar tendencies. I was advised to watch for those same symptoms as a result of my poor functioning liver and told to go to the nearest hospital should I exhibit them.

Only recently has the medical society realized that women may exhibit different symptoms from men both for similar diseases and in controlling medication. It had never crossed my mind to do a search of my mother's history and health until one spring when we were placing flowers on family members' graves. I couldn't find my maternal grandmother's grave. It had been an extremely muddy spring and the row markers had shifted. Barry joined me in my search. He asked what my grandmother's name was, and I said, "Vernitski," using the Polish pronunciation. I found it and shouted, "Here it is!"

He came over and said, "I thought you said, 'Vernitski' with a 'V. This says, 'Wernicka' with a 'W.'" Wernicka with an "a" denotes that the family member is female.

I explained the Polish pronunciation and was suddenly struck by the familiarity of the name to a German/Polish physician, anatomist, psychiatrist and neuropathologist whose name was given to a part of the left rear brain area called Wernicke's area. I had studied the parts of the brain in university but had never made the connection because everyone always pronounced his name and the area named after him as starting with a 'W.'

The area he studied is related to aphasia and is in the posterior hemisphere of the left brain. "Those with T aphasia can't understand words. They speak with regular rhythm and grammar. But the words don't make sense. They don't realize that what they're saying is nonsense."[19] Those afflicted with the condition have difficulty communicating.

Not only did I understand what I was reading, but I had also experienced it. When I was diagnosed with autoimmune hepatitis, a disease I knew nothing about, I was always asking what kind of symptoms I should be aware of that might signal a relapse. As mentioned earlier, being tired, black stools, yellowing of the eyes, but most of all, confusion. If I ever experienced mental confusion, I was to go straight to the emergency department of the nearest hospital. I always tried to be aware of what I said and how I said it. I noted throughout the last several years that as my medications increased or decreased, so did my ability to write and communicate. I became used to the fact

---

[19] Dr. Dan Brennan, May 20, 2021, WebMD

that I had to write, wait a day or so, and then reread the most recent pages. There were numerous times that I had to rewrite what I had previously documented to ensure that it made sense.

Genoswefa (Jean) Wengle, our mother, was one of the strongest women that I had ever known.

Her mother, whose name was also Charlotte, had left Jean and her two younger sisters with their father when they were in their teens. Jean raised her sisters but gave me her mother's name.

Jean had six children and lost one baby at eighteen months of age just before Christmas in 1944. The tree was up, and the floor was covered with gifts, some for the child who would not be there to celebrate. Never again would we see a Christmas tree decorated before Christmas Eve. When our brother Bob suffered his first heart attack in his early fifties, our mom said that she could not bury another child. She supported all her children, especially Sandra. She stoically accepted the blame for Sandra's behavior and provided support as Sandra moved from psychotic incident to psychotic incident.

When our dad drank and ran around, she made excuses for him. For years, I thought the Polish words, "eeshch to holetta" meant "go to hell." It would be two decades later before I learned that my mom was telling my dad to "go to his whore."

At fifteen years of age, after Dad had thrown a bottle at Joey but missed and fractured mom's cheek bone, I begged her to accompany me to family court and leave him. Her response was that our father needed someone to take care of him. She never shared her thoughts, but I know that she was thinking of her own dad who had died alone in a Toronto rooming house. She had married a man two years younger than her dad and she may have felt that she had failed our grandfather, but she wasn't going to fail her husband.

When our dad started displaying signs of dementia, Mom worked around the clock to keep him safe. She had an extra lock put on the inside of the apartment door. He learned how to escape. In the end, Mom couldn't even go to the bathroom without him exiting the apartment, travelling on public transit, and getting lost. Several times the police were called, and a search was initiated. He always explained that he had been riding the railway on his way to Chicago, something he did as a young man. Mom made all the arrangements for his admission to a long-term care facility and then called me to escort him.

Every Sunday was family dinner at our mother's apartment and every Sunday one of us was charged with the responsibility of picking up Dad and bringing him home so that he could enjoy the family interaction.

Three years after his admission, Mom had made all the final arrangements for his funeral before she called each of us to tell us that our dad had died. Seven years later, she had all the arrangements made for her own funeral before she died.

I developed a family tree combining both mental and physical illnesses. I have not taken this beyond my immediate family for two reasons. My initial investigation yielded enough information to warrant a more in-depth study than I was currently able to conduct. Records required to prove the mental and/or physical status of family members beyond my immediate family would only exist in Poland/Prussia or Germany. At the time my ancestors lived there, these documents would have been housed in local churches, many of which were destroyed during local battles to secure the now non-existent Prussia and/or during world wars.

I do believe that there is a gene that can cause some individuals to be susceptible to developing an inflamed brain that causes mental confusion. Did Carl Wernicke start his investigations in the area of aphasia when he discovered the part of the brain that deals with the ability to communicate, or was he investigating something else?

I believe that researchers are on the right track with their epigenetic studies. They are now looking for a trigger such as, "something ingested, like marijuana, or infectious, like bacteria." They "have come up with a variety of other suspects — head injuries, autoimmune diseases, brain inflammation disorder, parasitic microbes."[20] This is a huge advance from there just being a genetic link for mental illness.

I believe that there is a link between the increase in the number of individuals diagnosed as suffering from mental illness and the speed at which humans are evolving to cope with their ever-changing respective environments.

---

[20] Kolker, 320

Chapter Sixteen

FINDING YOUR NORMAL

The first thing everyone asks when I share my thoughts on this book is, "Just tell us, is it nature or nurture that caused Sandra's mental illness?" Then, "Is it nature or nurture that caused your physical illness?" It's time for society to closely examine the word normal in today's world.

To quote Evan Nesterak, the co-founder and editor-in-chief of *The Behavioral Scientist* (2017), "Asking which is more important, genes or environments, is kind of like asking which is more important in making an ordinary automobile run, spark plugs or gasoline." You need both. David S. Moore, in his book *The Developing Genome*, reveals that, "What counts is not what genes you have so much as what your genes are doing. And what your genes are doing is influenced by the everchanging environment they're in."

Evan Nesterak wrote that, "Epigenetic research demonstrates how genes and environments continuously interact to produce characteristics throughout a lifetime."[21]

"As soon as people start hearing … that your early experiences can have long-term effects," they do exactly what I did when I began my quest to find a sense of balance in Sandra's life. Everyone's first assumption is that they will be permanently scarred by a negative experience.

"Normal is a place I visit." [22]

The big concern is that we will pass any changes that our body experiences

---

[21] Evan Nesterak, *The Behavioral Scientist*, 2017
[22] Journal of American Medical Association, September 18, 1916.

on to future generations.[23] I worried that my children and grandchildren might experience either the mental or physical challenges that Sandra and I struggled to overcome. No one considers that there may be a possibility that people's "experiences might somehow improve the lives of their descendants."[24]

It's time to stop focusing only on the lifestyle and habits of those experiencing life challenges. Everyone needs to start realizing that when they look around a room, they will never find anyone who looks exactly like them.

We are all unique. Our genetic make-up and environments are unique. Our 'normal' is unique and it may change as we age.

If we look at individuals suffering from other chronic medical conditions that require pharmacotherapy, we will note how similar their challenges are. Those suffering from arthritis, hypertension, heart disease, irritable bowel syndrome, diabetes, lupus, cancer, and glaucoma all struggle with medication non-compliance.[25] Individuals suffering with mental challenges are no different from others suffering from chronic medical conditions, but those with mental challenges are often shunned, blamed, and criticized for trying to self-medicate.

My sister Christine, who suffers from heart disease, diabetes, and has bladder cancer in remission, is constantly hoping her doctor will reduce the number of pills she takes, thinking that if she gets off the pills, her body will return to "normal."

I'm no different or better. I may even be worse. Since becoming ill, I have a large Ziplock bag of pills to carry whenever we travel. My husband carries his medication in a medium Ziplock. I want to carry a medium Ziplock size! So, even though my head knows everything I am writing about, society norms pressure me to pour the larger pills into smaller bottles so I can use a medium Ziplock and feel that I am encouraging my body to return to 'normal,' whatever that may be.

Once my body started failing, my 'cocktail' included seven prescribed pharmaceutical medications and three supplements. Will that number be reduced? I don't know. However, I do know that my focus from today forward is not on eliminating medical supports; it's on finding the best possible combination that allows me to continue to live the life that I want at any age.

---

[23] Lamarck, pre-Darwinian biologist
[24] Evan Nesterak, *The Behavioral Scientist*, 2017
[25] Miklowitz, page 136

My focus with Sandra was to accept where she was. In later years, I knew that she would never return to what the world considers normal. I loved her the way she was. I only wish that I was more focused on every single medication that she was taking to ensure that her 'cocktail' allowed her to live the life that she wanted. I know that I appreciated her thoughts, her humor, and her kindness. She was and remained the glue that kept the family together. Even in her last years, her needs and care kept us communicating.

Many individuals turn to other remedies to deal with both physical and mental pain or angst. There is no concrete evidence that proves whether or not they are wrong or right. The concern is that when the individuals try to heal or cure themselves, they need to consider the interaction of their remedies with prescribed pharmacological recommendations.

Once conditions have been identified as having a genetic link (an individual carries the gene) with a biological cause (environmental), any stressor, positive or negative, can cause several chronic illnesses to express themselves. The study of "latent genes, activated by environmental triggers"[26] is called epigenetics and is a popular field of study today. The significant factor here is that, once identified, those illnesses or features of that individual are considered 'normal' for that person.

For example, any individual who has a predisposition toward high blood pressure may carry the gene for hypertension. If they lead a sedentary lifestyle and/or are overweight and experience either a positive (marriage) or negative (divorce) life stressor, they can develop high blood pressure, which would be considered normal for that individual and must be treated with medication to return their values within the safe range of functioning.

Similarly, someone born in Africa (environmental) and carrying the gene for sickle cell anemia (genetic) may express that illness by adding the stressor of moving to a high altitude. The individual is considered 'normal' with a disease.

People with diabetes and many individuals suffering from heart disease have a genetic predisposition to their illness, which may or may not express itself until a sedentary lifestyle, high fat diet, and age are added to a positive or negative life stressor.

Why are these individuals considered 'normal' and those suffering from mental illness considered abnormal?

---

[26] Kolker, page 320

An extremely bright young lady, Mathilde Brunet-Mercier, was recently featured on CBC's First-Person Story (July 22 ,2021) wrote about being diagnosed with Asperger's. She comments that the problem was never with the diagnosis but how 'impossible (it was) to achieve norms' that she had set for herself. She shares that she has been obsessed her whole life with being normal. "If you try to be normal when you're not, it simply will not work. It's like a fish trying to walk on dry land. It's literally impossible."

I believe Sandra and I had a close bond because I accepted her as normal. We still continued to look for ways to improve her situation. I noticed when people couldn't look at her withering body, but all I saw was her beautiful spirit. I have a filing cabinet full of notes, charges, pictures, meetings, prescriptions, caregivers, letters, and experiences. For the final eleven years of her life, I tracked her normal and we had a relationship.

In the process, I came to learn what I had been saying my whole adult life, "Listen to your body," and the fact that I am unique. My experiences are mine alone as are my illnesses. They may seem like other documented illnesses, but they are not identical. I learned to track not only my life story, but my medical history as well. I learned to be the conductor of my life and gave myself permission to be in control.

Rather than arguing and fighting with care practitioners or counting how many pills I must take a day, I'm comfortable saying, "This is my new normal." It includes physical activity, meditation, social interaction and a purpose, as well as food, pharmacological drugs, and over-the-counter vitamins.

I will speak up and share when I feel that what has been prescribed is not me.

I may say that a certain drug makes me dizzy. I need to take it at noon and not in the morning, because I need to walk or go to the gym and get it out of my system. Food and exercise change with trial and error and with age.

With the help of a team of medical professionals, I will monitor my 'normal' and refine it to allow me to live the best quality of life that I can in the years that I have left to enjoy.

In Sandra's story, she shared her demons, and she shared her struggles. She intuitively knew what her 'normal cocktail' needed to include. She walked. She tried to eat what her body needed. She took vitamins, prescribed medication, and additional medication of her own choosing. She did make sure that there was constant social interaction in her life as she tried to find that yellow brick road to balance and happiness. She was right to continue to try and suppress her demons. A year after our mother died, Sandra acknowledged that she wanted to live her life her way when she wrote:

<blockquote>
When I was young
And very carefree
All I thought of was fun
If they'd just let me be.
Years have gone by
I have lived my own way
Yet all the time I sigh
For my family wants it their way.
Don't do this
And don't do that
Presently I feel
Like the cat in the hat
A child again
At thirty-nine
Trying to pretend
That all is fine.
</blockquote>

It was the rest of us who tried to fit Sandra into a world of our making. Can you imagine how confusing that can be, given that each of our worlds are as unique as our fingerprints? It wasn't until I stopped trying to 'fix' her that Sandra and I were able to develop a strong and loving relationship. I learned more from her than she ever learned from me, but for the most part, whenever we were together, we enjoyed each other's company.

Someday the world will stop, really listen, and hear what those struggling with alternate views and demons feel and need. I know they try, but the world is missing the mark

Sandra and I were able to communicate because when we were together:

We lived in the moment. We discussed and acknowledged her world as real. Together we scheduled needed medical appointments. I arranged for her glasses to be fixed and joined her on entertainment outings, coffee runs and meals at restaurants. I asked about her friends, and we discussed our family.

I was able to look past the physical. If you remember my volunteer from the John Howard Society, I didn't change him. The environment I provided encouraged him to move closer to our norms. He didn't change. He still had bipolar tendencies, but he functioned better in a supportive environment, so did Sandra.

Sandra always felt that she belonged when our discussions moved into her world. I learned all about Freddie Fender and found that I really liked Tina Turner's music. One of Sandra's greatest gifts to me was a used tape of the French singer, Mireille Mathieu's songs. We both loved music. Sandra took piano lessons because I tried to learn. I struggled. She learned to play chords by ear.

I appreciated her intelligence, wit, humor, and insight. I was shocked at how much I learned from her.

Sandra's normal differed from mine. I learned from her, she learned from me, and we had a relationship. No one suffers from dementia, Alzheimer's, bipolar or schizophrenic tendencies 60 minutes an hour or 24 hours a day. Find the moments and build new memories.

Bravo to Simone Biles, Olympic gymnast, for saying "Enough, my normal has changed." Whether it's because of age, changing experiences, changing environments, or changing competitors, it doesn't matter. She took control and identified her new normal. I read that one young gymnast who competed five or six years previously commented that she never realized that it was an option or a possibility to say, "I can't go on."

We all struggle to be the best that we can be, but we must also remember that our best is unique to ourselves, and our best will change with age, illness, and world activities beyond our control. We need to be ready to accept when someone else's life is different. How they react may be different. Be kind. We are all in this life together. Don't try to be me and I won't try to be you. We can meet in the middle and still have a wonderful relationship.

Sandra wanted her body donated to science when she died. She wrote a reminder in her journal to, "Phone the University of Toronto about donating my body to science." (1995) I couldn't make that happen. Knowing Sandra, she would have understood that not all her family members were ready to make that decision. Sandra struggled with demons, but she loved her family. She would understand that people grieve in different ways, and she would smile and tell me to do what I had to do.

Sandra, know that you have made a difference for everyone who reads this. Someone, somewhere, someday will take this thinking further and discover that in actuality, we are all normal! The future challenge will not be to make us all the same but to acknowledge our differences and individual struggles as the world's brightest minds continue to investigate future possibilities that may advance world thinking and communication while reducing individual demons in this everchanging world.

www.ingramcontent.com/pod-product-compliance
Lightning Source LLC
Chambersburg PA
CBHW070831160726
48004CB00001B/336